Catherine's love of writing was cemented by her first poem being published in the school magazine. A few years later, she joined a publishing company, which enhanced her writing prowess. Desperate to work abroad, Catherine applied for and was accepted as a personal assistant in the Foreign and Commonwealth Office. Overseas, she enjoyed the unique experience of working alongside various Ambassadors. Shortly before retirement, Catherine was honoured with an MBE, presented at Buckingham Palace by the late Queen Elizabeth II.

To Shadow.

Catherine Joan Francis MBE

FOR THE LOVE OF ANIMALS

AUSTIN MACAULEY PUBLISHERS
LONDON · CAMBRIDGE · NEW YORK · SHARJAH

Copyright © Catherine Joan Francis MBE 2025

The right of Catherine Joan Francis MBE to be identified as author of this work has been asserted by the author in accordance with sections 77 and 78 of the Copyright, Designs and Patents Act 1988.

All rights reserved. No part of this publication may be reproduced, stored in a retrieval system, or transmitted in any form or by any means, electronic, mechanical, photocopying, recording, or otherwise, without the prior permission of the publishers.

Any person who commits any unauthorised act in relation to this publication may be liable to criminal prosecution and civil claims for damages.

All of the events in this memoir are true to the best of author's memory. The views expressed in this memoir are solely those of the author.

A CIP catalogue record for this title is available from the British Library.

ISBN 9781035889747 (Paperback)
ISBN 9781035889754 (ePub e-book)

www.austinmacauley.com

First Published 2025
Austin Macauley Publishers Ltd®
1 Canada Square
Canary Wharf
London
E14 5AA

A big thank you to my husband, John, for his help with putting this book together.

Part I
Birds

Chapter 1
Wild Birds

From an early age, I had a deep love of birds. Luckily, our garden was festooned with hundreds of wild birds. Cats were their main predator. When I found an injured bird, I took it to the nearest vet. This meant a return bus journey so my pocket money quickly evaporated.

Eventually, the bus conductors stopped asking me to pay; seeing my little cardboard box, they were aware I was on my way to see a vet. On the return journey (if the bird could not be saved), my tears said it all. I would receive lots of hugs from the conductors and the regular passengers plied me with chocolate and sweets.

My father was also an avid bird lover. One Saturday, as we strolled down the lane to my aunt's farm, he suddenly stopped, telling me to keep very still. Having ensured Mother Blackbird had left her nest, Father crept towards a hedge and eased some twigs aside. He urged me to have a quick look. I was totally amazed to see four mottled eggs lying in a beautifully-crafted nest.

We slid away and hid behind a nearby tree. Dad's main concern was that the blackbird may have spotted us and would abandon her eggs. After what seemed an age, barely daring to breathe, he gave a sigh of relief. Dad had just spotted 'Mum' flying towards the hedge, making a beeline for her nest.

Later that year, I caught the dreaded whooping cough and was confined to bed. As both parents worked late into the evening, the time passed slowly. Occasionally, various aunts came to visit, checking I was taking my medication. They were full of chatter about various fairs and events happening during the Christmas period. None of their enthusiasm took the edge off my glumness.

Luckily, our apartment was at the top of a four-storey building, which overlooked the Parish Church. The magnificent plane tree in their grounds was 'home' to several birds. On 'good' days, I sat by the window watching the birds flying back and forth, digging for worms and feeding from our bird-table.

As Christmas Day approached, my misery deepened. I was still very poorly and feeling rather glum. Tears of self-pity often trickled down my cheeks.

On Christmas Eve, everything changed!

Chapter 2
Cheeky

I heard my father opening the front door and put on a 'pretend' smile. Dad rushed over to my bed and, with a magician's flair, produced a tiny budgerigar from his pocket. He put the bird into my open hands. Being completely mesmerised and overcome with emotion, I barely heard his tale about how the bird had come into his possession.

First, Dad ran through the feeding routine. He had been given a bottle of liquid nutrition by the breeder who told him the bird would need to be fed every three hours. He asked me to choose a name, which would suit either a male or female. After some thought, I decided to call it 'Cheeky'. Dad told me the cere—the 'nose' above its beak—would be defined when the bird was six weeks old. If Cheeky was a male, his cere would turn blue (female ceres are beige). The breeder's instinct told him this was probably a boy. I did not care what gender it was—I just wanted to give the little darling all the love in the world.

Later that week, Dad related the whole story. A professional breeder had appeared in our local pub and was endeavouring to find someone who wanted to buy the bird. He told the assembled company that the budgie's wing had been damaged, when it broke out of its shell. It would therefore be banned from taking part in any 'shows'. Dad was having his after-work pint and overheard this sad tale. He tapped the breeder on the shoulder, telling him he wanted to buy the budgie.

Chapter 3
Bonding

After Cheeky had finished nibbling at his feeding bottle, this tiny bundle of feathers tucked itself into my bodice and fell sound asleep. I stayed awake all night, afraid I might accidentally turn over and flatten the wee one. When Cheeky woke up, the bird was eager for more food and finished the entire bottle. Christmas Day now looked like turning into a much cheerier occasion than anticipated!

Cheeky and I usually spent most of the day, lying in bed. This tiny bundle needed lots of sleep. Occasionally, we sat by the window and watched the wild birds flitting about. When we were tucked up in bed, Cheeky would fall asleep, lying against my cheek, or ease itself into my bodice for extra warmth. Winter's claws had struck and we had no central heating. (I was often in trouble for switching on the 'expensive' electric fire.)

A few weeks' later, I noticed a hue of light purple appearing on the cere. Now Dad was positive about its gender—it was definitely a boy. Later that week, Cheeky began responding to my chatter. I was convinced he was trying to talk. One morning, I clearly heard him say, 'I love you.'

My parents were astounded that such a young bird was starting to talk. When Dad told this tale to the breeder, he was quite overwhelmed. He deeply regretted he had not kept the budgie. In spite of his damaged wing, he believed Cheeky could have been the star of his Show.

When I was well enough to go back to school, Dad bought a cage and some toys for Cheeky. I hated leaving my darling boy. Every school morning, I kissed him goodbye, telling him I would be back soon. At lunch-time, I rushed home to give him a kiss and ensure he was not fretting.

Meanwhile, Cheeky began listening to my parents' chatter and astounded Mum and Dad when he announced, 'Whose turn to wash up?'

Chapter 4
Farewell Wee Boy

When I was seventeen, we moved to a more modern apartment. Cheeky quickly adapted to his new home, showing no fear of a change in circumstances. He had the run of the flat and frequently hid in my bedroom, so we could cuddle up together during the night.

Cheeky was really fond of Dad and often squeezed himself under his shirt collar for a sleep. This habit almost signalled the end of my wee lad.

Most weekends, Dad placed a small bet with the local book-keeper. On Grand National Day, there was a particularly long queue and it took ages for Dad to be served. When he, eventually, handed the forms over the counter a neighbour, standing behind Dad, tapped him on the shoulder and whispered, 'Do you know you've got a budgie under your collar?'

Dad said nothing in reply. He collected the betting slips, gave a brief nod, then edged his way to the exit. Slowly walking home, he carefully avoided meeting anyone who might recognise him, and want a chat. Cheeky now began shuffling around, making himself more comfortable.

Holding his breath, Dad carefully climbed the stairs to our flat, praying none of our neighbours would open their front door. Tentatively, he put the key in the lock, catching a glimpse of Cheeky peering over his shoulder. He quickly went indoors. The bird immediately spread his wings and flew straight to his cage—it was time for his seed!

Dad explained to Mum about his slow, tentative walk home—a truly nerve-wracking experience. He felt that he had just climbed Mount Everest. Mother gave him a large scotch to settle his nerves.

When I arrived home and heard this tale, I gave Dad a big cuddle, telling him he was a real hero. His knowledge of birds had been put to the test, and he had passed with flying colours. Had he tried to grab Cheeky, the bird would have panicked and flown away.

Four years later, when I was working in London, my darling Cheeky passed away. I cried for hours, remembering the happy times we had spent together, and all the fun and laughter he brought into my life and that of my parents. He was one in a million.

Apparently, the breeder, whom Dad still met occasionally, said he still despaired of ever finding a bird like Cheeky. Whenever he met my father, he said selling that bird was still preying on his mind. He doubted if he would ever breed another like him.

However, I was happy that Cheeky had enjoyed a good and happy life, was deeply loved, and had not spent his life being a 'show bird'.

Chapter 5
London

Although I was enjoying my work in the London Foreign Office, I was equally keen to be posted overseas. However, it was obligatory to spend a few months in the UK to get acquainted with the job, as well as find time to study at least one foreign language.

The buzz and continuous noise, that was London's trademark, was quite enervating. The quietest place, near my office, was St James's Park. At lunch-time, I sat on a bench near the pond, eating my sandwiches and revelling in watching all the different birds.

There were swans, geese, mallards and a platoon of ducks swimming contentedly in the various lakes which permeated the park. They quickly cottoned on to my habits, knowing I would share my lunch with them. Often, a plethora of sparrows would take turns to land on my palm and fly off with any peanuts on offer.

After spending six months in London, I was eventually posted to the European delegation in Brussels and, five years later, sent to the High Commission in Kuala Lumpur.

(All my overseas adventures will be detailed in Part 2 of a trilogy called 'My Beautiful Exploits'.)

My third posting was to Germany. Spinal problems prevent me from driving so I bought a bicycle and could now travel to work independently, without having the embarrassment of asking for a lift every day. (The embassy was far off the beaten track.)

After I worked out how the embassy operated, I tried socialising with my colleagues but found it difficult to fit in. Later, a few colleagues succumbed to my 'charms' and I established several long-lasting friendships. However, when I was alone in my flat, I continued to feel very unsettled and isolated.

On the spur of the moment, I asked a friend if she would take me to the best pet shop in Bonn, where I hoped to find a little bird who was looking for love.

Chapter 6
Starsky

In the shop, it took only a few minutes to reach a decision. First, I heard a rather loud 'cheep' and turned round to see a gorgeous budgerigar, who appeared to be giving me a 'wink'.

As soon as I drew near, the bird hopped onto his cage bars and stared into my eyes. I noticed his cere was already turning blue—a baby boy! His magical charm, and the gentle way he nibbled my fingers, were enchanting—perhaps we were meant for each other?

I immediately purchased the bird, a cage and other necessary accoutrements. The little lad was put into a ventilated box for the journey home.

During the drive back to my apartment, I thought about a suitable name for the bird. I went through several choices in my head. However, his sky-blue feathers eventually led me to the name 'Starsky'. My friend agreed this was an excellent name for such a beautiful boy although teased me about 'Hutch'—he would need to be found too!

As soon as I had settled Starsky into his cage, he headed straight for his seed dish. Later he fell sound sleep, leaning against his mirror.

When I returned from work, I would hear Starsky's welcoming cheep when I opened the door. My first priority was to start his training while he was young and malleable. I began by putting my hand into his cage, encouraging him to hop onto my finger.

When he had mastered this, the next stage was to let him out of his cage. First, I put him on my head and walked him round the whole apartment. Next it was time to encourage him to stretch his wings.

After some hesitation, he soon mastered the art of flying and began zooming around like a mini-tornado. His 'landing' abilities were more of a challenge.

Nevertheless, Starsky's determination and perseverance won the day. My life now had a new meaning and loneliness became a thing of the past.

A few weeks later, I was certain he was trying to talk and positive I heard him saying his name.

Chapter 7
Starsky Goes to Work

I hated going to the embassy and leaving Starsky alone all day. With some trepidation, I asked my boss if I could bring my bird into the office, assuring him he would be no trouble to anyone.

This kind-hearted man looked at my woebegone face and nodded his permission.

My bicycle had a basket attached to the front of my bike so I bought a smaller version of Starsky's cage, which would sit firmly into this space. Every (dry) day, I put Starsky in his travel cage and cycled to the office, putting his cage on a table, alongside my desk. Starsky quickly settled into this daily routine and appeared to enjoy 'going to work'.

Later, he began making a 'clacking' noise. Eventually, I realised he was copying the noise of my old-fashioned typewriter! Starsky was very popular, even my boss was smitten. I will never forget that, while fixing one of his toys, he decided this was more important than attending the ambassador's morning meeting. The head of mission was not amused.

One lunch-time, I took Starsky to the canteen. The chef, Hans—a tall, rotund man—did not suffer fools gladly. I was a little concerned he might not be happy with a little 'Vogel' (bird) in his restaurant. Hans wandered across to our table and, instead of throwing us out, sat down and pushed some lettuce through the bars of Starsky's cage. We chatted away for ages in a mixture of English and my basic knowledge of German.

I overheard some muttering in the background. Several people were saying the bird was 'contaminating' the premises. Hans also overheard these comments. He stood up and made a loud announcement—the gist of which was, that anyone who had issues with the bird's presence, could leave now, and would be banned forever. There were no other restaurants in the vicinity—the canteen was the only option. Every lunchtime, Hans always made time to bring Starsky a treat and sit down for a natter.

Most weekends, a friend invited me for a drive in her new car. Starsky was welcome, too. When we stopped for a snack, I put his cage on top of our table. He was in his element if someone came over for a 'chat'.

Occasionally, a dog would be interested, too, and would press its face against his cage. Undaunted by such behaviour, Starsky would give any dog who designed to do this, a nip on the nose. This usually had the desired effect and the dog would slope away.

Chapter 8
Leaving Germany

Due to the fact that Bonn is below sea-level, the vertigo I had suffered for several years, became unbearable. I would often stagger and fall. This meant riding a bike was now impossible. The local doctors were excellent and arranged for various hospital visits.

However, there was no cure or medication available to help. It was going to be a long haul to find a solution to this particular problem. Following a consultation with my boss, agreement was reached that I should leave Germany and seek help with my balance issues in the UK.

My main concern was how to get Starsky back to Britain. However, luck smiled on me, as it turned out that a member of the embassy knew my parents. Steve told me he had been born in my home town and, very kindly, agreed to do all he could to help with the officialdom involved in arranging Starsky's transportation.

When I left Germany, Steve said Starsky would stay at his home. When all the bird's travel documents were in place, he would make arrangements for him to be flown to Scotland.

A few days later, I returned to London, then travelled north to live with my sister and family. My maisonette, in

London, would have to remain on a rental basis until I had a solution to my vertigo problems.

After a few nail-biting days, an agent based at Glasgow Airport, telephoned to say that Starsky had arrived. My brother-in-law, Raymond, agreed to drive me to the airport. During the journey, I could barely breathe—I was so excited about seeing Starsky again.

We arrived at noon and informed that the storage area was locked for lunch.

Chapter 9
Red Tape

Ray returned to his car to wait. I decided to investigate further and did a tour of the airport. Inside the terminus, I spotted a flight of stairs—possibly leading down to the storage area? The first few doors I came to were locked. Finally, I found one that was open and crept inside, praying no one would see me. This enormous shed was piled miles high with a multitude of suitcases, crates and boxes.

I began calling for 'Starsky', with the faint hope that my voice would carry some way across this mega-sized building. Nothing. I tried again and again, shouting louder each time.

Eventually, I heard a faint cheep.

Repeatedly calling his name and following his little chirps, I found him. Starsky's cage was sitting on top of a large suitcase, surrounded by various crates. I clambered over several boxes and eventually reached his cage. He was overjoyed to see me and began chatting away, non-stop, no doubt telling me about all his adventures.

We were on our way to the 'Exit', when two officials appeared. They said I could be arrested for breaking into a 'restricted' area. Tears flowed down my cheeks. Wiping my eyes, I explained that the door I entered was not locked, adding that my wee bird's presence would hopefully help me recover from an illness, sustained in Germany.

The officers had a long conversation. Convinced I was going to be taken to jail, I began to tremble. A few moments later, the men escorted me upstairs. Instead of taking me to prison, they took me to an office, telling me this was where to pay Starsky's transport fees. They waved 'goodbye', wished me lots of luck and, to my great surprise, one chap blew Starsky a kiss!

When all the forms and payment were completed, I tapped on the window to alert Ray that we were ready to go home. Knowing I was prone to fainting, he thought my 'wave' indicated that I was about to keel over.

He slammed the door shut—which locked the car automatically—and bounded up the stairs. When he saw me holding Starsky's travel cage, ready to go home, he dashed off (in a bit of a temper), trying to find a way to 'pick the lock'!

Chapter 10
Starsky in Kilbirnie

Starsky quickly made himself at home. At 'playtime', he was the star attraction. My youngest niece, Gaynor, bought him a miniature, wooden castle which he was eager to explore. However, his first love was a small plastic ball. When someone opened his cage door, Starsky would pick up this ball, from the bottom of his cage, and throw it out. Then he flew down and began tossing his toy around the room.

Whoever was looking after Starsky would have to endure his shrill calls at playtime if he lost his precious ball. Anyone looking through our ground-floor window would have been amazed to see several children and adults, crawling around the floor, peering under chairs and searching behind the curtains, all frantically searching for a plastic toy.

When I was alone with Starsky and let him out for a fly, his preference was to sit on my finger and listen to my chatter. He also picked up a whole range of new words, repeating phrases he had picked up from the family. One day, he clearly said, 'Where's that bl…y Budgie?' (Maybe, he had been listening to Ray?)

During the summer, we all went for a holiday in the Highlands. We had been invited to stay with friends in their newly-acquired hotel. It was agreed Starsky would be welcome, too.

Apparently, the owners possessed two large dogs, whom I was keen to meet. Perhaps I could take them for a walk in the surrounding countryside?

On arrival, we gathered in the hotel lounge. I placed Starsky's cage on the coffee table while we chatted with our hosts. Both dogs wandered over to have a closer look at this strange object. Intrigued, they pressed their faces against Starsky's cage.

At this point, my boy decided to teach them a lesson and bit both their noses! Both dogs quickly slid away to the safety of the kitchen. Later, I took the dogs for a country walk, trying to make amends for Starsky's 'naughty' behaviour.

A few months later, I was called back to London, to take up a new post, and was also informed that the office had arranged an appointment at a 'Benign Vertigo' clinic.

My sister promised Starsky would be well looked after. Nevertheless, I also planned to travel to Scotland most weekends.

Chapter 11
Starsky Takes to the Sky!

There was a near tragedy when Starsky managed to escape. One warm summer's day, my sister had taken him outside, to join the children in the garden. She was attempting to attach a bath to Starsky's cage when he squeezed over her hand and escaped. First, there was a stunned silence, then all the children cried in unison, 'What will Aunt Catherine say?'

(I was in the middle of a three-day course in London at the time and only heard this tale a few days later.)

Starsky was apparently enjoying his freedom! He was zooming around the heavens, darting in and out the clouds, like a small tiger moth.

Suddenly, he spotted a flock of crows heading towards him. Starsky decided to make for home. He flew straight down, diving deep into a hedge, bordering the garden. Everyone kept very quiet, pondering on what to do next.

Various ideas were proposed on the best way to catch him, then quickly rejected. My niece, Carolyn, took matters into her own hand. She slowly crept towards Starsky's hiding place, holding his little mirror, and manoeuvred her hand through the foliage. No one dared speak. Everyone was holding their breath, watching intently as Carolyn brought

Starsky out from the hedge. He was now sitting on top of his mirror, chatting away as usual.

Carolyn walked tentatively towards his cage. With admirable aplomb for a youngster, my niece manoeuvred him back into his cage, where he immediately went to play with his plastic ball.

All the family cheered—a dreadful tragedy had been averted!

Chapter 12
Farewell Wee Boy

During one of my visits to Scotland, I was concerned to see that Starsky was looking a bit out-of-sorts. As there was no obvious indication as to what was wrong, I thought he was just about to moult.

Shortly after my return to London, my sister rang to say that Starsky looked unwell and she had made an appointment with the vet.

Apparently, during the trip to the surgery, Starsky became very agitated, then appeared to fall asleep. When the vet examined him, she said the wee lad had died. It later emerged that Starsky had suffered a stroke.

My sister telephoned with the sad news. My heart constricted with pain as we reminisced about Starsky's many adventures. I relived my time with him in Germany and recalled all the adventures and happy times we enjoyed together.

He was such an amazing wee boy.

I was so thankful he had not been lost somewhere in the deep blue yonder (as nearly happened) and was with family members when he passed on. Starsky was nine when he died—a good age for a little budgerigar.

His empty cage in the sitting room in Scotland brought everyone to tears.

'Goodbye, darling boy. We will all miss you, and your amazing chatter, so very much.'

Photo 1—Starsky

Part II
Marriage and Travel

Chapter 13
Saudi Arabia

In 1989, I was posted to the embassy in Saudi Arabia. At first, I felt very lonely—recreational pursuits were not encouraged by the Saudis, making it difficult to socialise. One day, I overheard my colleagues discussing a bridge club and I asked if my basic knowledge of the game would permit me to be accepted into this group.

I was encouraged to participate. Members of the club played 'Chicago Partnership Rotation'. Basically, this meant two players moved to a different table after completion of the rubber. One night, a rather handsome man rotated to my table and sat opposite me. He was going to be my partner for this particular game. My bridge hand was well-balanced, with several high cards. I therefore made an opening bid of 'one no trump'. My partner (John) immediately jumped to 'seven notrumps'—the highest bid in bridge. I choked violently, glaring at him furiously. After a tense game, sweat trickling down my back, I eventually made the contract and almost fell off my chair with sheer exhaustion. I vowed never to speak to this man again.

A few months later, I invited three friends round for a game of bridge and supper. One guest dropped out at the last minute—I urgently needed to find a fourth player. No one sprung to mind. What to do? Panicking, I eventually managed to track down the chap I met at the bridge club.

'Could you come around this evening for a game of bridge?'

He was somewhat bewildered, thought for a few moments, then said, 'Okay. Where and what time?' I gave him the information.

The bridge evening went well and everyone seemed to enjoy themselves. At midnight, guests began to drift away. John was also about to leave. I stopped him in his tracks. 'You can't leave yet. You are on washing-up duties to make up for my nerve-wracking experience at the bridge club.'

A few weeks later, we agreed to go out for dinner. Soon our friendship blossomed into a romantic liaison.

Bizarrely, after few months, John asked for my hand in marriage and, even more bizarrely, I accepted!

As he was working with the Saudi government and I was at the embassy, we had to be circumspect regarding our relationship. Our meetings were few and far between. In September, we managed to organise leave from our respective bosses to visit the UK. Our plan was to 'warn' both our families of the forthcoming nuptials.

Prior to the date of our departure, the Iraqis decided to invade Kuwait and, together with the threat of nerve gas and scuds aimed at Riyadh, it was a tense time for everyone. By the skin of our teeth, we managed to book seats on the last remaining plane to leave Saudi for the foreseeable future.

After a night 'chilling' in a London hotel, we travelled to Wales, where I met John's parents, then drove up to Scotland.

John was introduced to my sister and family and, that afternoon, asked my mother if she would bless our marriage. Fortunately, Mum welcomed John to the family. (He 'joked' that she skipped around the sitting room with glee!) Other comments were that John deserved a medal and my youngest niece said, 'He's a brave man!'

Chapter 14
Marriage Preparations

At the end of September, we returned to London and enjoyed some time together before John returned to Riyadh. Our next meeting would be in March, a few days prior to our wedding. (My own contract in Saudi had already been terminated by the ambassador.)

As my maisonette in Dulwich was sorely in need of upgrading, the amount of work involved would stop me pining too much. I also had the opportunity to meet up with old friends and socialise with my London colleagues. Most weekends, I travelled to Scotland to begin preparations for our wedding.

As well as helping my nieces choose bridesmaids' dresses, I arranged to see the minister about the Order of Service and book a date for the reading of the banns. I also managed to reserve an excellent organist, and found an accomplished soprano, who kindly agreed to sing two arias during our wedding.

My worst nightmare occurred when a member of staff, at our chosen reception venue, telephoned to say that we 'must' find a different date for our 'party'! Apparently, they had double-booked for that particular day. I was horrified. All the wedding invitations were in the post and John's boss had already promised him three weeks' wedding leave. Panicking, I rang my fiancé. His advice was to make a strong complaint to the hotel manager. If he tried to force me to find a new date for our reception (which he did), I should inform him that our solicitor would be in touch to demand compensation for the extra expense and distress. This did the trick. The date for our reception was hastily reinstated.

Our Scottish wedding took place on 9 March 1992 and was followed by a delightful honeymoon in Arran. Shortly after our return to London, John was obliged to return to Saudi to complete his contract. The days dragged by slowly as we counted the hours till we could be reunited.

After six months, we had a delirious reunion and were so happy to be a team again. We spent many hours exploring everything London had to offer and, at weekends, travelled to the coast and paid frequent visits to John's parents.

Out of the blue, I was offered a posting to Bulgaria. Perhaps not our ideal venue but we relished the challenge. Now, there was the usual flurry of packing and finding tenants for our maisonette.

Chapter 15
Italy and Greece

Shortly before Christmas (1992), we set off on our 'eventful' journey. In spite of having to manoeuvre our way through blinding snowstorms, our drive through Europe was relatively smooth. However, when we reached Italy, everything changed and we hit major problems.

During an overnight stop in Milan, our estate car was broken into and our large trunk stolen. During the burglary, one of the front windows was smashed. As it was New Year's Eve, all garages were closed and would not open again for several days.

To make matters worse, when we arrived at the Port of Ancona, we discovered our reservation had been cancelled—apparently, our particular ferry had been chartered by a wealthy Italian (for a private trip).

There were two options. We could either risk a treacherous three-hour journey, through a blinding snowstorm, to the Southern Port of Brindisi (where another ferry would depart several hours later), or spend two nights in a local hotel, awaiting the next ship to leave Ancona.

We opted for the one and only hotel. This was probably the wrong decision. The bedrooms were freezing, there was no hot water and the dining room was closed. (Fortunately, the railway station had a restaurant which provided reasonable meals.)

Two days later, we finally boarded the ferry. On arrival in Greece, we drove for several hours, trying to find an 'open' garage. On the car radio, we heard there were huge snowstorms in Bulgaria. It was now even more urgent to replace the window.

I wondered if any garages were open.

Despair was setting in when, thankfully, in Thessalonica (close to the Bulgarian border), we eventually found a garage with a sign saying 'Open for Business'.

After explaining the problem, the owner sent one of his workmen to scour the town, in an attempt to find the correct window glass. Thankfully, he succeeded. When the job was done, we were told there were no upmarket garages in Sofia; replacing the window in Bulgaria would have been nigh impossible.

It was now late evening. We were advised by our 'mentor' to find a hotel for the night as another blizzard had been forecast over the Bulgarian mountains.

Chapter 16
Journey to Bulgaria

The following morning, as we were driving towards Bulgaria, I began to panic—sweat was trickling down my back. John looked at me enquiringly, wondering if I was feeling unwell. My problem was my fear of telling him that my navigation had gone awry, and we were actually én route to Turkey! In the end, I had no option.

Scouring the map, I sussed out a 'mountain route', which would bring us in the direction of Serres—the border town in Bulgaria where we had planned to spend the night, before heading towards Sofia.

This mountainous route turned out to be somewhat quirky. The road arced up and down and there were no overhead lights. Several times we bounced off a steep slope, which threw the car sideways, and involved John in a lot of manoeuvring to get us back on track. We were really concerned that the road might become totally impassable. My greatest fear was that we would be stuck in the car all night. I was beginning to panic—the decision to try this route could turn into a major disaster.

Finally, we saw a glimmer of overhead lights in the distance. An hour later, we reached the main road and, thankfully, turned towards Serres. Just as we were about to enter the town, we passed a huge hypermarket, which looked brand new. Perhaps this would be the ideal place to replace the goods we lost when our trunk was stolen?

After enjoying a relaxing night in a hotel, we returned to the hypermarket and filled two trolleys with an assortment of electrical goods and bedding. I remarked that if we had taken the proper route to Bulgaria, we would never have found the hypermarket.

Although John agreed, he was also grimacing…

Chapter 17
Sofia

When we reached Sofia, we were struck by an aura of drabness—even the snow looked brown and dirty. People, wrapped in several layers of clothing, were struggling over the ice, most of them searching for an open shop or market.

We had the total luxury of being booked into the Hilton Hotel, waiting for our promised apartment to be vacated. We soon discovered that the excellent hotel meals were in total contrast to what was available in other restaurants around the city. ('Dish of the Day' was often 'Brains'.)

We went to the embassy to confirm our arrival and I told my new colleagues about our hazardous journey across the mountain. Everyone burst out laughing! Apparently, this route was still being built and not yet open to the public. (Perhaps a traffic sign should have warned unwary travellers!)

Chapter 18
Town Life

Five days later, our apartment was available, the previous occupant now having left for her new posting. This flat was on the thirteenth floor of a tower block and, sadly, the lift was frequently out of action. My back was becoming extremely stressed with tackling the stairs several times a week. There were also frequent electricity cuts and, occasionally, no tap water.

We wondered if country-living would be a better idea. John had a word with my colleagues and discovered there were several villas up for rent, on the outskirts of the city. As he would not be starting his own job for several weeks, John had time to visit various places to determine whether there were any suitable houses available. In mid-February, he eventually found a villa that ticked the majority of our boxes.

In March, we vacated our dreary apartment and set off for our new abode. Our new landlord, Valeri, and his wife welcomed us to their home. They hoped we would enjoy life in their villa.

Valeri warned us that living on the outskirts of the city also had its problems—mainly burglaries. There were other hazards as well, particularly during the winter, when roads were blocked by drifting snow. Overhead street lighting was very spasmodic plus there were the usual power and water cuts.

Our landlord had a few tricks up his sleeve. As there was a well in the garden, Valeri had installed a hand-made connection, meaning water could be fed into the loft tank—a cold shower would be better than none at all! There was also a wood burner in the garage, which would keep the central heating pipes hot if we had a power cut.

Valeri mentioned that, living on the outskirts of the city, we were prone to burglaries. We therefore asked the embassy to arrange for security grills to be fitted to all the windows and doors.

Sadly, these measures failed to deter determined intruders and we were robbed twice during our stay in Bulgaria.

Chapter 19
Country Life

We were enchanted by our new home and its surroundings. Ambling through the fields or driving to the top of Mount Vitosha soon embroiled us in country life. There is no industrial farming in Bulgaria, which meant birds, bees and butterflies were left in peace to swarm around the meadows—just as they had been doing since time began.

I began to think it might be a good idea to purchase a dog to give us an incentive to go for longer walks. By chance, I overheard office colleagues discussing new-born puppies (American cocker spaniels) available for sale. This was too good a chance to miss. We quickly made a date to visit the breeder.

At just six weeks old, all these puppies were adorable. However, one struck us as being more curious and playful than the rest. After some thought, we decided this was the puppy we really wanted. The owners were delighted, saying we could collect her in two weeks' time.

'Have you decided on a name?'

Blondi sprung to my mind. The colour of her coat was pure white, tinged with a hint of latte. I suggested this name to John and he agreed.

The big day arrived—it was time to collect our puppy. We were absolutely delighted with our bundle of fur—it soon became apparent that she loved to be loved. Blondi adored people and, even those who were not particularly 'dog-friendly', were won over by her gentleness. We also discovered that she could be naughty and stubborn and very clever at getting her own way.

Like all puppies, she adored 'stealing' things, especially slippers, and when one chap leant over the garden fence to pat her, she jumped up and snatched the pipe from his mouth! It took several treats before she dropped her special 'prize'.

Chapter 20
Rolos

One morning, John was obliged to pay a visit to a company on the coast, near Varna, and had to leave at dawn to catch his plane. I ordered a taxi to take me to work and was preparing a packed lunch. Accidentally, I dropped a tube of Rolos on the floor. Quickly, turning around to pick them up, I saw, to my horror, Blondi and Rolos disappearing down the steps into the garden.

Aware that chocolate could be fatal for dogs, I raced outside and managed to trick Blondi indoors with the offer of some treats. My strategy worked but she did not bring the Rolos. I opened the door again and she raced outside, probably planning to retrieve the sweets. Dashing after her, I eventually cornered Blondi at the foot of the garden. She now began squeezing behind the shed. Unable to reach her, I reluctantly went back to the kitchen.

While meditating on what to do next, Blondi ran back to the house, holding the chocolates between her teeth. Once again, I tried and failed to retrieve the sweets. Blondi now ran to her favourite hiding place—a tight space behind the bookcase.

Knowing she ought to see a vet, I began to panic. There was no point in requesting a day's leave. Yesterday, we were informed that it was essential that all staff should endeavour to get to work, as an emergency was looming. My taxi was already at the gate.

At present, Blondi showed no symptoms of being ill. However, if she ate all the chocolates, I knew this could change. Eventually, I had no option but to leave Blondi to her own devices and said a little prayer that she would not succumb (or even die). If she was ill when I returned home, my only hope was that there would be a surgery still open.

After a strenuous working day, and my constant worry about the puppy, I was near to breaking point when it was time to leave the office. Seeing my distress, a colleague kindly agreed to give me a lift home. As soon as I opened the front door, Blondi rushed towards me, then ran into the sitting room. She retrieved the mangled packet of sweets, dropped them at my feet, then went to find her toys.

Only one chocolate was missing from the pack. Either she did not really like Rolos or this was her way of making amends.

Tears ran down my cheeks. I sat on the floor playing games of fetch with the little rascal. Blondi was totally mesmerised by receiving so many cuddles and kisses!

When John returned, I related the whole story. Although he was concerned about Blondi and her possible demise, he could not help laughing at my 'Tale of the Rolos'.

Photo 2—Blondi

Chapter 21
A Lost Kitten

Blondi loved being in the garden and 'helping'. One weekend, it dawned on me that she would sit and stare through the fence for hours on end. Why? There were few people passing by and not many dogs in the vicinity.

The answer came to me later that week—Blondi was waiting for a cat to appear. I remembered she became really excited when she saw one passing our gate. Maybe I should have a chat with John to discuss the possibility of buying a kitten?

Events overtook us. One autumn evening, when John was taking Blondi for a walk around the village, he noticed a neighbour's two large dogs—Rocco and Aldo—were running free. The dogs were barking noisily and trying to squeeze under a stationary vehicle. John peered under the car and spotted a tiny kitten, tucked behind the rear wheel. The wee one was mewing and shivering with fright. With the offer of several treats, John enticed Rocco and Aldo back to their own property, then firmly closed their garden gate.

Blondi had also spotted the kitten and was trying to squeeze under the engine. John asked her to 'sit and wait'—

amazingly, she complied. He then manoeuvred himself under the chassis and wriggled his way towards the little dot.

The kitten was very frightened and began hissing. Speaking softly, and with lots of coaxing, John managed to scoop up the bedraggled bundle, then carefully extricated himself from beneath the car.

He tucked the little one into his top pocket. Our house was only a hundred years away but it was starting to rain and the temperature suddenly dropped. Anxious to prevent the cat from succumbing to hypothermia, he quickly made tracks for home. Blondi was pulling on her lead, urging him to go faster. As soon as they arrived, John called, 'Surprise!' and produced a kitten from his top pocket!

Chapter 22
Tinkerbelle

I knew the little mite would be desperate for food. However, all the local shops were closed. Unable to buy kitten food, I had to come up with something and decided to make scrambled eggs. The kitten gobbled up every morsel.

Blondi now took charge and began mothering the wee one. She encouraged the kitten to 'pee', gently pushing it towards a newspaper. Blondi then enticed her charge towards a blanket. Our puppy was in love. She cuddled up to the kitten, gently wrapping her paws around its tiny body.

The following morning, John knocked on our neighbours' doors, asking if anyone was missing a kitten. He had no success. We phoned our landlord, explained the whole story, and asked him if he could check further afield, while we were at work. He telephoned that evening, saying his search had been fruitless. It appeared we had acquired a cat!

Knowing it was impossible to stop Blondi interacting with the kitten, a check by the local vet was very urgent. Luckily, we managed to get an appointment the following evening. The vet gave the kitten a thorough examination and, given the circumstances, pronounced 'she' was in reasonably good health.

He asked if we had decided on a name.

After a few moment's thought, I said, 'We'll call her Tinkerbelle.' (This was the name my aunt (who ran a farm with her husband) named one of her many cats. When this particular kitten was born, it was so tiny it could fit into a small coffee cup. I recalled telling Aunt that, if I ever had a cat, I would call her Tinkerbelle.)

When we were leaving with our new charge, the vet said that he was looking forward to seeing us again. 'Perhaps, you'll bring a goat next time?' he chortled.

Chapter 23
Chaos

We decided to come home every lunch-time to check on the kitten. On the first occasion, we were unable to track her down. After searching the whole garden, we began to think she must have wandered back to her old home.

Blondi was curled up in her basket at the top of the steps, outside the front door. I went to give her a cuddle and was amazed to see a soggy bundle of fur, cradled between her paws. She must have been licking Tinkerbelle all morning. Her large tongue had almost drowned the wee one. Nevertheless, this 'licking' had kept the kitten's circulation moving. If the mother cat had been around, she would have done the same—albeit more gently!

As the months passed, Tinkerbelle turned into a beautiful cat. She was a feisty wee thing and had a spirited nature. Every day, the pets fought playfully for hours on end. When Blondi settled down for a sleep, the kitten would creep up and jump on her paws. Then she danced off to her own little refuge, mewing squeals of delight.

In the spring, the pets romped through the garden, crushing my daffodils and snowdrops. Next door's cat (whom we called 'Sinbad'—being unable to pronounce his Bulgarian name) jumped over the fence and joined in the fun.

A few months later, Tinkerbelle was itching to join John and Blondi when they went for a stroll. When we thought the time was right, John took both pets for a walk.

Tinkerbelle was now in her element. She loved roaming through the woods, chasing the butterflies and bees, and literally anything that dared move!

Chapter 24
House-Party

We decided to repay the hospitality we had enjoyed, by inviting our colleagues and friends to a garden party. We were delighted when one lady brought her dog. However, Tinkerbelle was not amused. Quick as a flash, she raced towards this interloper and chased the poor dog into the street! Fortunately, the owner quickly retrieved her pet, while we attempted to catch our little terror. (Over the years, we discovered Tinkerbelle hated all dogs—except her beloved Blondi.)

John carried Tinkerbelle up to the study. From the balcony she could view the assembled company and—more to the point—the visitor's dog would be safe from her claws!

The sandwiches and desserts quickly disappeared. The sun shone all day and we were so pleased no one showed any inclination to leave.

One of our guests, Rumen Statkov (a very talented artist) wanted to see Tinkerbelle. I watched as he sketched our curled up cat, sound asleep on a chair—he also added a little bell to his drawing to personify her name.

By early evening, people started drifting away. We were very tired but happy that the day had been a success, pleased that all our efforts had not been in vain. Now the clearing up began …

Chapter 25
Holidays

Throughout Bulgaria, there were so many interesting places to visit—Plovdiv (an old historic town) and the Black Sea resorts were top of our list. Also, being within reach of Greece, was an added bonus particularly as there were several supermarkets dotted around. Before going home, we always bought a wide range of food to stock up our cupboards.

Blondi charmed everyone. In one Greek restaurant, she was given freshly cooked lamb, which looked a lot more tender that the meat we were given!

During a visit to a beach club, by the Black Sea in Varna (Bulgaria), a trio of singers serenaded Blondi. She sat quietly on my knee—mesmerised and totally bemused.

During that particular holiday, we were invited for a tour of a Navy Ship. Blondi was also given permission to accompany us. Sadly, when we were invited below deck, the puppy was obliged to remain on the upper deck. Although reluctant to leave Blondi, we had to comply with the rules.

Unhappily, we leashed her to a bollard.

When we returned, we found Blondi running around the deck. Apparently, several crew members ended up having tug of-war games with Blondi, using various ropes—she was thoroughly delighted with all the fun and attention.

Apparently, she had not missed us at all!

Chapter 26
Where's Tinkerbelle?

Valeri warned us that we were in for an exceptionally cold winter. He came to the villa to ensure the wood burner was in good working order and checked all the pipes were properly lagged. He also informed us the water tank (fed by the well) was filled up to the brim.

As winter began to tighten its grip, we were concerned when Tinkerbelle did not appear for her evening meal. She was always on the prowl so assumed she had found a good scent. When Blondi began to fret, John took her for a walk, in the hope of finding our little cat. Their search was fruitless.

Blondi refused to eat her dinner. Midnight approached and still no sign of Tinkerbelle. Our concerns deepened, especially as it was starting to snow.

It was a long, arduous week. Blondi was in deep despair. By Thursday morning, we began to lose hope of finding Tinkerbelle alive—the overnight temperature had now dropped to minus twelve centigrade.

The next morning, after clearing the snow from the drive, we waited in the car, while the engine warmed up, before setting off for work. I looked towards the kitchen window and saw Blondi's sad face peering through the glass.

Tears trickled down my cheeks. My poor darling. The love she had for Tinkerbelle was etched on her beautiful, woebegone face. Wiping my eyes, I glanced once more at Blondi and blew her a kiss.

John was just about to drive off when I yelled 'Stop'. I had just spotted Tinkerbelle rushing up the outdoor steps, heading for the kitchen door.

We ran across the snow-laden garden, carefully avoiding slipping on the frozen ice. We skirted round large snow-drifts then raced up the steps towards the door. I quickly scooped Tinkerbelle up in my arms, putting her inside my coat for much-needed warmth.

Meanwhile, John was frantically struggling to open the front door—in the last few minutes, the lock had frozen solid. After what seemed an interminable time, he eventually succeeded. Gently, I placed Tinkerbelle on the kitchen floor so she could run to Blondi, who was barking with delight that her much loved soul-mate was finally home.

Tinkerbelle quickly gobbled up a whole tin of cat-food, then wolfed down a plate of chicken and sausage. Blondi stood by her side, patiently waiting till she had finished every morsel. A few minutes later, they cuddled up together on the sofa.

Why had Tinkerbelle disappeared? How did she survive the cold? Maybe she became trapped while out hunting? We were aware that most suburban home-owners only paid weekend visits to their villas, to undertake general maintenance. Perhaps last weekend, a neighbour, inadvertently, locked her inside his garage before heading back to town?

If what we surmised was true, Tinkerbelle would have spent four long days and nights—cold, lonely and hungry. We would never know the truth.

Fortunately, Tinkerbelle made a quick recovery and, two days later, the pets resumed their mad games of chase throughout the house.

Life was back to normal!

Part III
The Far East

Chapter 27
Bulgaria to Italy

In mid-June, I was posted to Jakarta in Indonesia. It was really sad saying goodbye to our colleagues, and the many friends we had made in Bulgaria. However, it would be intriguing to live in a far eastern country again.

Before we were married, the Foreign Office posted me to Malaysia—a fascinating place which embraced a variety of ethnic communities. When John was serving with the Royal Navy, duty took him to Singapore—he was overjoyed with the news of our next posting.

Our expected arrival date in Jakarta was early December. This meant a six-month gap. Where was the best place to look for a rental home? Animal quarantine in the UK was still in place and, not wanting to be separated from our pets, we opted for France. From there I could easily access London by train. (The office having already arranged several Bahasa lessons in Whitehall—apparently knowing how to speak the native language was essential.)

I remembered that a colleague owned a second-home South of Paris, near the Loire Valley. After phoning to explain the circumstances, she very kindly agreed to let us rent her cottage for the foreseeable future.

As we would be taking the pets with us, we needed to find the quickest and easiest route. After pouring through several maps, it seemed the best option was to drive to Greece, pick up the ferry to Venice, book a hotel—possibly near Cremona—before driving into France.

First, we drove through Bulgaria, heading for the Greek port. After a three-hour wait, we were finally allowed on board. Previously, we were informed that Blondi would be allocated a crate on the ship's upper deck. As we had visitors' rights, we would be permitted to bring her food and walk her around the decking. Not much fazed Blondi. During the voyage, she adapted to these unusual circumstances and soon found her 'sea-legs'.

It was sad that Tinkerbelle had to remain in the car. Fortunately, we were permitted to check on her regularly, and always found her sound asleep. After dinner, we retired early to bed, conscious of the long journey we were about to undertake.

Sailing into Venice was quite spectacular. The architecture and magnificent buildings, which gradually came into view in the early morning, crepuscular light were stupendous. Nevertheless, it was a great relief when we were all tucked up in the car, ready to begin the third phase of our journey.

Chapter 28
To France

Given it was mid-summer, it was fortunate we had already reserved a hotel room in Cremona. On arrival, we were delighted to see this was actually an old chateau, surrounded by fields and vineyards.

The manager showed us the rooms available—either a superb suite, draped with silken curtains, or a small villa next to the swimming pool, which was less ostentatious. We opted for the latter. Silk curtains would be a disaster if Tinkerbelle decided to claw her way up the drapes!

We spent the rest of the day lounging by the pool, then enjoyed a delicious meal in the chateaux's 'dungeon' restaurant. The following day we took Blondi for a wander around Cremona. During our walk, we learned so much about the history of Violins. Later, we were fortunate to find a bistro that welcomed dogs.

The next morning, we set off on the final lap of our journey.

Finding our way through the French countryside was tricky—especially as there were very few road signs. Fortunately, John's map-reading was first-class. When we reached our destination we were tired, hungry and longing for sleep.

First, I needed to feed the pets and unearth all their bedding (and ours) from the car. Meanwhile, John was collecting logs for the fire—although mid-summer, it was a bitterly cold night. After finishing the sandwiches bought at a local bistro, we collapsed into bed.

The pets had a great time in France. They adored going for long walks in the nearby lanes, meandering through the surrounding fields and playing games of chase in the woods.

Blondi particularly loved going on picnics, especially if there was a little stream nearby where she could have a paddle.

Chapter 29
Chaos

One very hot morning, Tinkerbelle jumped through our bedroom window, with a huge, male cockerel clenched between her teeth. Total chaos ensued. I threw a towel over the pair and managed to get a good grip on Tinkerbelle. After a frantic struggle, John succeeded in prising the bird from Tinker's tightly-clenched jaw. He carried the cockerel over to the window and gently dropped him on the ground.

The bird ran like the wind towards the nearest field. We quickly closed the shutters—to stop our little terror chasing after her 'prize'—then tumbled back into bed. Tinkerbelle quickly cuddled up between us, purring contentedly!

In spite of my various train journeys back and forth to London, we were still able to enjoy several local excursions. There were an abundance of chateaux in the vicinity plus a plethora of restaurants, serving excellent food.

In late October, I received a letter, giving me a date for the start of my posting. The first priority was to start making travel arrangements for the pets. This was a complicated process. First, they needed to be taken to Paris, where they would be thoroughly checked by a vet, prior to their flight to Jakarta.

Sadly, it could take several days for travel permission to be granted.

By coincidence, we knew a lovely couple, working at the Paris embassy, who were besotted with animals. After appraising them of the situation, they kindly agreed to care for our pets in their own home. They also arranged for a local vet to give Blondi and Tinkerbelle a health check. If Blondi and Tinkerbelle passed their medical tests, the vet confirmed that arrangements would be set in hand for their travel to Jakarta.

Our own plan was to set off for Jakarta as soon as possible. It was essential to collect the pets as soon as they arrived at the airport.

Chapter 30
Jakarta: Blondi and Tinkerbelle's Arrival

Five days after we arrived in Jakarta, we were ecstatic to learn that Blondi and Tinkerbelle had arrived. With my boss's permission, we immediately set off for the airport.

We were furious to learn that the handling agents for Air France had not forwarded any of the pets' paperwork—no airway bills, original passports or even health certificates. The official in charge point-blank refused to release the pets. Dripping wet, thanks to the steamy heat, we argued with all the officers for three long hours.

Eventually, the top man cleared the pets through Customs on the strength of the photocopies we had of their passports (it also helped when I mentioned I was attached to the Embassy). John was then told to see an official at their head office to arrange for the original pet documents to be forwarded immediately.

At last, we were then granted permission to see the pets. I was horrified that neither had any access to water—the dish attached to Blondi's crate had disappeared and the cat's water container was totally dry. We were permitted to rehydrate

Blondi but told not to open her crate. She was going crazy to get out but had to wait till we were all back in the car before she could launch herself into my arms.

Peering into Tinkerbelle's crate, we were alarmed to see she had a very serious problem—her pillow was soaked with blood.

When we reached home, I fed Blondi then bathed Tinkerbelle's front paw, covering the wound on her foot with a small sock. Meanwhile, John was ringing our colleagues, asking if anyone knew the telephone number for the nearest vet. As this was an emergency, he was advised to contact the animal hospital. Unfortunately, Reception had just closed so he would need to wait till morning to make an appointment.

Tinkerbelle ate some tiny morsels of food then headed for bed—our bed! Curled up in a ball, she soon fell fast asleep. Blondi recovered quickly from her long journey and, with our friends' agreement, we took her to our 'welcome party'.

Blondi was the star of the evening, adored all the attention and charmed everyone—even people who were wary of dogs fell in love with her. She was a real 'ice-breaker'!

The following morning, we composed a letter of complaint to Air France, asking for compensation for their lackadaisical attitude to pets in transit. A few weeks later, we received a reply. Air France denied everything. However, they enclosed a token amount of money for our pets' distress.

Chapter 31
Tinkerbelle's Operation

The following morning, John was given an early hospital appointment for Tinkerbelle. Sadly, I was obliged to go to work. Blondi was being looked after by our staff. She had quickly wormed her way into their hearts. It is unusual for Indonesians to become close to pets—particularly dogs. However, they were unable to resist Blondi's special charms.

At the office, I waited impatiently for John to telephone. Finally, he rang. Sadly, Tinkerbelle needed a major operation.

The diagnosis was a shattered claw and a broken knucklebone. It would be a delicate procedure as part of the toe joint had to be removed. She would have to stay in hospital for at least three days. A nurse would ring when she could be collected.

We were trying to work out what had happened to our poor cat. Perhaps the roaring engine noise during lift-off terrorised her. Or maybe, she broke her toe while scrabbling at the door of her carrying cage? If only pets could talk!

John collected Tinkerbelle three days later. Her leg and foot had been bandaged in a large dressing. When the painkillers wore off, she began to howl with pain. With difficulty, we administered two more tablets. Lifting her onto my lap, I stroked her gently in an effort to keep her calm. An hour later, she fell asleep.

On Boxing Day, Tinkerbelle's stitches were removed. She could now hobble around and was able to cuddle up to Blondi. Tinkerbelle's new game was chasing any geckos that came within her radar. I was relieved that she was coming back to her normal, mischievous behaviour.

Both pets quickly settled into a new routine of going for a cool evening stroll instead of their usual habit of having an afternoon walk. Blondi even enticed dog-wary Moslems to pat her head. However, most of the local community were totally astounded to find our cat tagging along too.

We were grateful that both pets acclimatised quickly and soon adapted to the very humid environment.

Personally, I found the heat and humidity very hard to bear.

What joy to have an air-conditioned office!

Chapter 32
Life in Indonesia

Our first task was to find new accommodation. Our allocated home was a disaster. In fact, the whole place needed a proper uplift and completely new furniture. As he did in Bulgaria, John once more accompanied several estate agents around town, trying to find a house which suited our needs—and preferably one near the office, so we could return home at lunch-time to check on the pets.

Again, he was lucky in his quest and found a well-appointed house within walking distance of the Embassy. Sadly, it lacked a swimming pool. This was a pity, as my back needed lots of exercise. We were fortunate that several colleagues, living locally, invited us to have a swim in their own private pools.

A few months later, John was offered a job at the consulate, next door to my office. Work permitting, we could both go home every lunch-time to check on our mischievous rogues. We usually found them wrapped around each other, asleep on the sofa.

The constant worry was that nearly every day, there were protest marches by thousands of disenchanted people. Civilians often marched through the streets, demanding the overthrow of whichever president was in power and, occasionally, a bomb-blast would rattle the windows— terrorising everyone. Even more frightening, many hotels, shops and buildings were set alight. Soon smoke began smothering the horizon.

To offset this madness, we were fortunate to have the opportunity to escape to the Puncak Mountains. The office had rented a large villa (for use on a rotation basis), to enable staff and their families to unwind.

Another location was a beach-hut in Lombok, which was large enough to accommodate two families. Across the Java Sea, you could see the Son of Krakatoa, smouldering in the distance.

A longer excursion was to a bungalow at Pelabuhan Ratu where the Pacific Ocean waves gently lapped at the shore. There was the added bonus of a restaurant at the far end of the lagoon, which served great food. You just had to ignore the rats scampering in the rafters!

These weekend trips, often with friends, rejuvenated and helped us cope with whatever madness we had to face on return to Jakarta.

Chapter 33
The Puncak Villa

Our favourite getaway was to the Puncak Villa. We loved wandering through the tea plantations, meeting the local people and practicing our scant knowledge of the local language. Blondi adored going to the Puncaks. There was a huge garden stretching all around the villa, which embraced a large swimming pool.

At first, we decided not to take Tinkerbelle, concerned she might become disorientated and decide to run away. However, matters were decided when we were packing for a Puncak weekend break and discovered Tinkerbelle already sitting in her cat-box—something she never did voluntarily! (Strangely, if we going to either of the two other resorts—which had no secure fencing—she somehow knew and had no issues with being left behind with the staff.)

Tinkerbelle adored the fresh mountain air and loved wandering through the villa grounds, frequently carrying tentacled creatures around the garden. Another game was to sit by the swimming pool and 'bat' any sleeping frogs into the water.

One evening, just as we were finishing dinner, for some reason John looked up and was horrified to see Tinkerbelle walking along the rafters. If she fell, she would probably break her neck as the beams were close to the top of a very high ceiling.

With a lot of coaxing and the offer of several treats, our mischievous cat decided to make her descent. Jumping from the beam, she clung on to a large curtain and slid down to the floor. Totally unperturbed, she tucked into her dinner.

Later, we sat outside, having a drink, watching the setting sun sinking below the horizon. Totally exhausted by the torturous drive up to the Puncaks, weaving our way between hundreds of other cars heading in the same direction, we soon headed for bed.

Naturally, both our pets decided to snuggle in beside us.

Chapter 34
Safari Park

Near the villa was a large safari park. We were told by the local people that the park covered several acres of land, all interspersed with a medley of streams and rivers. The added bonus was that dogs (inside cars) were also permitted.

The first time we visited the park, Blondi was sitting on my knee, peering through the partially open window. We stopped the car, having spotted elephants and their calves nearby.

The youngsters were having a great time—playing and splashing about in a small river—while the bull elephants were in the process of uprooting various trees. (Later, we learned that all this wood would be used as shelters or playthings for animals kept in enclosures.)

I lowered the window a little more so Blondi could get a better view of the elephants. A few minutes later, a llama sauntered towards us. It stretched its tongue through the window and began licking Blondi's head!

In her usual laidback way, Blondi appeared totally unfazed by this close encounter with a strange creature. The llama meandered off, seemingly quite pleased with itself—

maybe it had been waiting for the opportunity to nuzzle a dog for a long while!

We drove through the whole park, being fortunate to see lions, hippos and giraffes cavorting and meandering in a large fenced-off enclosure. When we arrived at the Baby Zoo, we were permitted to leave the car and go for a wander.

In one area, a ruined temple overlooked a huge pool where water gushed from the surrounding caves. Large white tigers were enjoying games of 'chase', leaping across the boulders, and fighting playfully in the water. Occasionally, they would become aggressive and lash out, using their huge paws as weapons. When they tired of this 'game', the tigers made their way into the caves to curl up for a siesta.

In another area, you could have your photo taken with the 'tamer' inhabitants. I opted to do this and sat in an enclosure with three adorable white (baby) tigers, who decided to have some fun at my expense. After posing on my knee for a photo to be taken, they began pulling and tugging at my clothes. With my hair and attire now the worse for wear, I opted to move to a 'quieter' pen and sat with an adolescent male tiger sprawled across my knee.

I felt perfectly relaxed and the tiger also seemed very calm. However, when he spotted someone outside our enclosure wearing a red jacket, he became very grumpy. When his growling intensified, I began stroking him gently murmuring words of comfort. In spite of my efforts, his irritation markedly increased. The keepers decided it was time to take him back to his pen in case he went into attack mode.

My last animal encounter was with a family of adorable orangutans. I sat beside 'Daddy', while Mum stood behind me, putting one of her huge arms around my shoulder. Their darling baby opted to sit on my knee, cuddling up against my chest, simultaneously trying to dislodge my necklace.

Needless to say, I did draw the line at getting close and personal with the very dangerous Komodo Dragons!

Photo 3: Author with family of orangutans

Part IV
Belgium

Chapter 35
Brussels

During 2003, five years after suffering the turbulence of life in Jakarta, we were posted to Brussels. In 1972, my first posting was to Belgium. I was aware this was a very cultured city with an abundance of good restaurants, museums and parks. John studied the map and noted there were many forestry areas too. Here, Blondi would be free to romp around and paddle in the little streams, which appeared to criss-cross through the woods.

We were allocated our predecessor's home, within walking distance of several restaurants and a nearby park. This house had three storeys—garage, living room/kitchen and two bedrooms. The sitting room was above the garage and the kitchen balcony overlooked the garden.

Our first priority was to collect the pets from their boarding kennels. Blondi had been allocated a small room, with another dog, and they seemed to have bonded already. Searching for Tinkerbelle, we eventually found her roaming around a fenced enclosure.

When the fees had been settled, we quickly bundled the pets into the car, eager to show them their new home. (The owner told us Blondi's kennel-mate was being picked up later that morning, so her companion would not have much time to fret.)

We decided to keep Tinkerbelle indoors for a few days until she was familiar with her new abode. (This was the advice in the 'Cat Lover's Companion'.) Meanwhile, Blondi was eager to have a romp outside.

After admiring the garden, and trying to identify some of the many flowers, for some reason, I looked up at the house— horrified to see Tinkerbelle trying to squeeze through the balcony railings, all set to launch herself into space!

John dashed upstairs and managed to catch our kamikaze pet before she jumped. We decided it was safer to let Tinkerbelle join Blondi in the garden. Obviously, some cats needed to be kept indoors for a few days to familiarise themselves with their new territory. Tinkerbelle made up her own rules!

After the pets had bounced all over each other, they set off to explore their new domain. Later, we found some outdoor chairs, then enjoyed a welcoming glass of wine. The unwinding process was now underway and we could begin putting behind us all the organisation and stress of travelling halfway around the world.

The pets loved their new garden and soon curled up on a towel I unearthed from my suitcase. To protect them from inclement weather (while we were at work), the next task was to install a dog flap.

A job for John!

Chapter 36
Hospital

During the winter, I felt desperately ill and was admitted to hospital on two occasions. Apparently, the stress and anxiety of five years in Indonesia had caught up with me. After being discharged from hospital, I still had to take a plethora of medication every day, none of which alleviated any of my strange symptoms.

Towards the end of the following year, the FCO informed me that the medical adviser (MA) urgently needed to see me. I travelled to London the following day. We had a long discussion. Following this, the MA said the best idea would be to request medical retirement, which he would endorse.

A few weeks later, I was informed that my contract had been terminated and I should make plans to leave Brussels at the beginning of March.

It was really sad, albeit inevitable, that our stay in Belgium would be curtailed. We had been looking forward to exploring more of the surrounding countryside, as well as visiting the nearby towns and villages. However, this was not to be.

We were also becoming increasingly worried about Blondi, who appeared to have various health issues too. Our local vet was very concerned and instigated several tests.

In January, he told us the results indicated Blondi had breast cancer and that her prognosis was poor. Various medications were prescribed to control her pain. However, he emphasised that Blondi was unlikely to survive beyond a couple of months. We went into total shock. It took a long time before we were able to accept this dreadful diagnosis.

Every lunch-time, we struggled home from work, weaving through the usual chaotic traffic jams. We needed to ensure Blondi was not suffering and to comfort Tinkerbelle—who instinctively knew her 'mum' was unwell.

It was a very stressful time. The only way to cope was to keep calm and be strong for both pets.

Chapter 37
House-Hunting

The next pressing matter was to find a retirement home. After a long discussion, we decided to start our search in southern France. As I would be leaving the office in March, we would need to begin house-hunting soon. Who would look after the pets while we were away?

Happily, our maid, Janine, agreed to 'live-in' and take care of both animals. She said she could manage this for a week, adding she would be delighted to have the pets to herself.

We were also aware a British couple, who had bought a second-home near Poitiers, were on holiday in the UK. We eventually tracked them down and asked if we could stay at their villa for a week. They kindly agreed and point-blank refused to accept our offer of rent.

Before establishing ourselves in our friends' house, we picked up some groceries and then began tracking down house-agents. The next morning, we did the rounds of several estate agents and were taken to see various properties. By the afternoon, my symptoms reared their ugly head and I felt seriously unwell. Sadly, John would need to view any other properties alone. When I started to feel a little better, I began pouring through several house-brochures.

It was a nail-biting time. None of the properties John visited were anywhere near the criteria we had set ourselves. In four days, we were due to return home and were becoming quite frantic. The next afternoon, while scouring through yet another 'Homes for Sale' brochure, I came across an advert for what appeared to be our ideal home. John agreed this property could be the answer to our prayers.

He immediately rang an estate agent and discovered the villa was still on the market. The agent told him this was a lovely house, built on the outskirts of the small town of Exireuil. The property was surrounded by acres of countryside and only a mile away from two supermarkets. We arranged to meet at the villa early the next morning.

It did not take long to agree that this was our ideal home. There were three bedrooms and two studies plus a huge garage below the house, which also had a cave for wine. The current owners were including a tractor in the selling price. (Why did we want a tractor?)

It turned out that a tractor would be necessary to cut the grass in the large meadow—the big field at the rear of the house. The agent added there was also a tree-covered hill at the foot of the garden, so we would always have plenty of firewood.

We walked around the property, noting that only a small amount of renovation was needed to the house, plus some of the outbuildings were a little dilapidated. However, no major work was involved.

The next day, we signed all the documents with the local lawyer, then headed back to Brussels. An exhausting trip but well worth the effort.

Chapter 38
Blondi's Last Days

In the middle of February, Blondi began to go downhill rapidly. We were devastated when the vet advised us that her prognosis was now very poor—perhaps she might last for another week, he said, brushing a tear from his eye. Blondi had wormed her way into his heart too.

We were acutely aware that Blondi's pain was becoming too much for her (and us) to bear. She had stopped eating a few days previously and was now urinating blood. It was, with great reluctance, that we asked the vet to arrange for Blondi to be put to sleep, preferably in her own home.

A date was set. Meanwhile, he asked us to try to keep things normal and be calm. Easier said than done.

We tried to make Blondi's last day very special. We picnicked at her favourite place in the countryside. Here, she could wander through the woods and meander along the little paths beside a tumbling stream. In the more open area, I vividly remember kneeling on the ground, opening my arms wide, and calling her to, 'Come to Mummy!'

Blondi ran like the wind, as if she was flying up to heaven itself, and launched herself into my open arms. Tears ran down my cheeks. Blondi snuggled against my chest, then raised her head and stared into my eyes. I think she knew in her heart that soon she would be in God's arms. Another angel in heaven.

So that Blondi would be more comfortable, I sat in the back seat of the car, holding her steady. (We had already stopped using her seatbelt in case it exacerbated the bleeding from her tummy.) When we arrived home, John carried Blondi up to the sitting room.

Blondi refused the offer of any food or treats. Once Tinkerbelle had eaten, they cuddled up together on their favourite blanket, quickly falling asleep.

The vet arrived the following morning.

Chapter 39
Farewell, Darling Blondi

Our vet made a big fuss of Blondi, then gave her an injection to make her sleepy. She was very frail and, after a little snuffle at his medical bag, Blondi headed for her blanket and closed her eyes.

We were told to keep talking to Blondi, as she could still hear us. We cuddled up to her, reminiscing about all her overseas adventures, being acutely aware that Tinkerbelle was watching intently. She was sitting on the sofa, gazing avidly at her 'mum'.

A few minutes later, we were asked to go into the kitchen. The vet was now preparing an injection to stop Blondi's heart. He indicated that Tinkerbelle should also leave the room. However, she raised her bright, green eyes, staring at him defiantly. It was almost like she was stamping her foot and telling him, in no uncertain terms, that she was 'definitely not leaving her mum'.

We went into the kitchen and held each other tightly. We prayed Blondi's passing would be gentle. A few minutes later, the vet knocked on the door informing us that Blondi had died. We went back to the sitting room to say our final goodbyes.

The vet had wrapped Blondi up in her favourite blanket. We kissed her little face and many tears dropped on her head.

The vet said he would take Blondi back to his surgery and arrange for a personal cremation. He would inform us when her ashes were ready for collection.

Tinkerbelle was still sitting rigidly on the sofa, her piercing green eyes having absorbed everything. We think she knew, deep in her heart, that Blondi would not be coming back. I tried to explain that Blondi's suffering was now over. Tinkerbelle gave me a strange look before careering upstairs to our bed.

The next morning we received a personal letter from the vet. He said all the surgery staff were very sad we had lost Blondi. She had really touched their hearts and was such a brave girl during her last few months.

He wished us to be strong…

During this sad time, although we were both grieving, we still had to tackle packing up and preparing for our imminent departure to France. However, there was a more pressing problem to address. Tinkerbelle had stopped eating and howled all day, and most of the night, like a demented banshee.

She paced around the house, searching for Blondi in every corner. Her constant wailing continued day and night. She was in acute distress—just as we were. Eventually, I asked the vet to prescribe her sedatives. Not our preferred course of action, but we were badly in need of sleep.

After a few days, Tinkerbelle responded to the medication and at last began to eat a little food. Occasionally, she would jump onto my lap, curl up, and have a nap. At night, she crawled into our bed and slept alongside John.

It was going to take a long time, and a lot of patience, to bring her back to the feisty wee cat we knew and loved.

# Part V
France

Chapter 40
The 'Tail' of a Beautiful Dog

In late March, after all the ups and many downs, we set off for France. The car was heavily loaded (and also had a trailer attached). Tinkerbelle was somewhat distressed, not knowing what was happening, and began pawing at her crate. As soon as we arrived at the villa, we set her free. Rejecting the offer of food, Tinkerbelle scampered off to investigate her new surroundings.

Several hours later, Tinkerbelle reappeared, ate some supper, then curled up on our bed. After unloading a few essentials, we also managed a light meal before retiring.

The following day, the rest of our baggage arrived from Brussels. We spent several hours unpacking and rearranging the furniture. Later, we sat on the patio and made a list of all the items we needed to buy. We also needed a new aerial—the one left behind had fallen off the roof and was lying in bits on the patio.

During our shopping expedition, we arranged for various workmen to come to the house. The following morning a man in overalls turned up. Without any chitchat, he went straight to work. (He brought with him an extendable ladder, so we assumed he was going to replace the broken aerial.) When he had finished the job, I offered him some refreshments.

While we were chatting, he mentioned that, while on the roof, he had spotted a cat. He said it was sitting on the front drive, next to a motionless six-foot snake. Racing around to the front of the house, we found Tinkerbelle sitting beside her 'prize'. The handyman told us this was a Slow Snake and quite harmless, in spite of its size. We felt so sorry for the poor creature.

Before long, Tinkerbelle returned to all her mischievous ways. She was often seen carrying around various tentacled, creatures or picking up multicoloured lizards. One day, a salamander gave her a nasty bite. Fortunately, we got her to the vet in time and they were able to flush out the poison. However, Tinkerbelle did not learn from this dice with death and continued foraging in the bushes and rampaging through the wooded area, searching for more prey.

We also joined a French language class—a great way of getting to know our English and French compatriots.

The good news was that the fresh country air and the lack of stress were really beneficial to my health. After a few months, I felt much stronger and began embracing the delights of our country walks. During these exploratory rambles, we also managed to track down various riverside restaurants.

However, we desperately missed Blondi's company. It would have been delightful to have taken her on our various excursions. Tinkerbelle is a great companion but, as the distinguished author, Gerald Durrell, quoted, 'A house without a dog is not a home.'

Photo 4: Tinkerbelle in France

Chapter 41
Abandoned Puppies

After careful consideration, we concluded we really wanted a dog, preferably one who desperately required a loving home. Friends told us that there was an animal sanctuary in Dordogne. We enquired about buying a lovely-looking puppy, which appeared on their website. However, we were too late—this dog was snapped up very quickly. The people in charge later emailed us. Apparently, six abandoned puppies had been found and were being cared for at a farm, close to their headquarters.

We asked for some background. Apparently, when out for a walk, a man spotted two dogs lying close together, appearing to be in some distress. He slowly edged towards them, astounded to see that the bitch was in the process of giving birth to a litter of puppies.

Being totally spooked by someone approaching them, both parents ran off, abandoning their litter. This kind-hearted man picked up the puppies, cradling them inside his jacket, and took them home. He then contacted the police, hoping for some advice. He was told to keep the puppies warm and wait till an officer arrived.

Two policemen arrived and took the entire litter back to the station. A senior officer decided to contact a vet to come to the gendarmerie and euthanise all the pups!

A female member of staff became quite distressed about what was being proposed and secretly decided to contact the animal sanctuary. Two senior members immediately went to the police station, demanding the puppies should be released into their care.

After a long heated debate, with lots of shouting on either side, the pups were handed over to their 'saviours'. The sanctuary was due to close for two weeks, while the owners went on vacation. The puppies were therefore being fostered at a local farm.

We were really moved by this tale and asked if there was a female among the litter. The farmer's wife told us there was one female and four males. As we wanted to have a bitch, there would be no hard decisions to make. We quickly agreed a date when it would be convenient to visit the farm.

Chapter 42
Whisper

Reaching the Dordogne, and positive we were in the right area, we were still unable to find the farm. We came across a local man, who pointed us in the right direction. Arriving forty minutes later than expected, we made our apologies to the farmer. He gave a Gallic shrug when he heard our tale then took us into the yard. We saw lots of puppies running around in a fenced enclosure. All the dogs appeared to be enjoying themselves—play-fighting and bouncing over each other. We tried but failed to identify our hopefully soon-to-be puppy.

The farmer's wife invited us into the farmhouse. She told us 'Whisper' was smaller than her male siblings and was constantly being bullied by them. Plus, all the other dogs joined in this 'game' too. Madame went off to collect the puppy.

We waited with bated breath, then heard the door creak. Madame returned holding Whisper in her arms.

When she put the puppy on the floor, this tiny wee dot ran behind the sofa and, for about ten minutes, remained in her hiding place. Meanwhile, we chatted about the sanctuary, saying how lucky the puppies were to have been rescued. The sound of our voices began to intrigue Whisper.

I watched as Whisper tentatively emerged from her hiding place, gradually edging towards my feet. Bending down to pick her up, I put Whisper on my knee. After some hesitation, she began snuggling into my lap, then licked my hand. I was totally smitten with this bundle of fur.

Whisper needed love. We could offer her a comfortable home and, perhaps in time, she would forget her bad start in life. I looked at John for approval. He seemed a little unsure at first. Seeing tears welling up in my eyes, he eventually nodded his agreement. Madame was delighted. While we were chatting about the puppy's current diet and any established routines, the little one fell asleep. After paying and completing all the forms, we waited while Whisper was given a bath, then John carried her to the car. I sat with Whisper on the backseat, giving her the opportunity to move around. However, she preferred my lap and soon fell sound asleep.

We were travelling along, making good time, when the weather turned itself upside down. Heavy rain, bolts of thunder and jagged streaks of lightening, struck us from all angles. Unable to see the road, John drew onto the verge. Visibility was now zero.

Thirty minutes later, the rain eased off and a glimmer of sun peeked from behind a cloud. We could now continue our journey.

Whisper was snoring quietly when we arrived home.

Chapter 43
Whisper Renamed

As soon as we arrived, I carried the puppy into the sitting room and took her out to the patio. Gently putting Whisper down, I knelt beside her, hoping she would start absorbing her new surroundings. I was totally startled when the puppy shot off, running like a rocket, straight towards the lily pond.

Racing like the wind, I quickly reached the pond. Whisper was now struggling to keep her head above water. Thankfully, I managed to get a grip on her collar before she disappeared completely.

I wrapped Whisper in a warm towel. John rushed to help and was startled when he saw a drenched puppy, shivering with fright. Rubbing her dry, I held her firmly against my chest, feeling her heart racing in time with my own. Later, when she calmed down, I encouraged her to play with Blondi's toys then put her on the sofa, where she curled up for an afternoon siesta.

After supper, I carried Whisper into our bedroom, placing her on a blanket alongside our bed. She appeared content with this arrangement and soon drifted off to sleep. The next morning, I found her lying on her back, tossing her little teddy in the air.

Tinkerbelle crept across the bed and peered down at this tiny bundle of fur. She stared at the puppy for a long time, then gave me a piercing look. I think she was wondering what on earth we had brought home!

The next day, I walked Whisper across the meadow, trying to acclimatise her to our domain. She appeared fascinated by everything—this was her first encounter with trees, shrubs and wildflowers. Whisper sat stock-still, happily absorbing all her new surroundings.

Sadly, her early experiences had made Whisper wary of men. Despite several attempts by John to play with the puppy, she became snappy and one day bit his leg.

During our walks, I contemplated on the best way to help Whisper and John to bond.

A few days later, we decided we wanted to change her name. John said 'Shadow' suited her best, as she followed me everywhere. I read in one of my puppy books that the best way to get a dog accustomed to a new name was to sing to them.

When we went for our daily walk, I would sing (rather badly):

You are my Shadow, my only Shadow,
You make me happy when skies are blue, You'll never know, dear, how much I love you, Please don't take my Shadow away.

After a few days, the puppy began responding to her new name and 'Shadow' was put on her pet passport.

Chapter 44
Shadow Learns to Swim

Tinkerbelle slowly began to interact with Shadow, one day bringing her a dead mouse. She watched as the puppy, unsuccessfully, tried to eat her 'gift'. Shadow reciprocated by biting the heads off various flowers, dropping them near the cat's paw. Tinkerbelle would have preferred something she could eat, but accepted the gift with as much grace as she could muster. Although such a feisty cat, she also had a generous nature.

One day, searching though the bookcase, I came across a very informative puppy book. I now knew the best way to help Shadow and John bond. Apparently, he should take over the feeding regime and accompany us on our daily walks. After a couple of weeks, this had the desired effect and, slowly, they began to trust one another.

Thankfully, we could now all go for a walk together. One day, after strolling through the meadow, we ventured into the wood. Shadow was in her element, running through the bushes and scrabbling in the undergrowth. One day, I came across a colourful and very unusual plant tucked behind a tree. With the help of my flower book, I managed to identify this specimen as Viper's Bug-loss.

Shadow was still attracted by our pond and one day dragged out all my precious lily pads. Stupidly, we tried to catch her. Shadow began racing all over the garden, scattering the flowers everywhere.

A few days later, we bought her a paddling pool. Her attraction to the pond now began to wane. As we had been unable to save the lilies, we bought artificial ones, which looked quite attractive. Our resident toad seemed to prefer sitting on those rather than the real ones!

A few weeks later, we took Shadow to the local reservoir. Here she could paddle in the water and dig in the sand. On the second occasion, John decided to see if she could swim and threw her into the water, way out of her depth. I was furious—and frantic—terrified she might be pulled under by the strong currents.

Shadow completely disappeared below the surface. By now, I was panic-stricken.

Suddenly, Shadow's head appeared and she began paddling towards the shore.

'Well,' John said, 'at least she knows how to swim!'

Chapter 45
Football and 'Find Mummy'

Shadow became obsessed with her new tennis ball. One of her favourite games was playing at being 'goalie'. All visitors were 'obliged' to play footie with her. The ball would be plonked on a lap and her appealing brown eyes melted the sternest heart. This passion for 'football' lasted her entire life.

One morning, Shadow began ripping up Blondi's cuddly toys. I gently asked her if she would leave 'Chuckles' alone. I wanted something to hold when I was thinking of Blondi. (Chuckles was Blondi's favourite toy and, along with Tinkerbelle, all three would squash up together in their favourite basket.) Shadow never touched Chuckles again, even if the toy was within her reach. For a young puppy to be so astute, this was quite incredible.

Shadow's favourite game was, what we called, 'Find Mummy'. John would take her deep into the wood, while I found a hiding place—usually at the other end of the meadow, squashed behind a tree or bush. Then he would shout, 'Find Mummy!'

Shadow exceeded all expectations and, no matter how good a niche I had found, she would hurtle through the wood, making a beeline for my hiding place.

(She never forgot the words 'Find Mummy' and I had reason to be grateful for this several years later.)

Situated at the top of a nearby hill was a small maze. The first time we took Shadow, she was totally confused and unable to track down my hiding place. However, she eventually worked things out, in her own inimitable style, and appeared to relish this new challenge.

We decided to socialise Shadow by taking her into town and encouraged her to greet the local people. When we stopped for coffee, Shadow would lie by our feet. She soon became used to the cafe ambiance and appeared to relish these excursions.

Strangely, while driving into town, Shadow used to whine non-stop. However, on the way home, she was quiet as a mouse.

(It took several months—and a trip to Spain—before we discovered why this happened.)

Later, we ventured further afield, taking Shadow for various picnics in the countryside, and often took her to Niort, where there was a small park. There she could have a paddle in a little rivulet which ran through the grounds.

On one occasion, when we visited this park, we had a dreadful fright—a huge Rottweiler, walking alongside his owner, decided to run straight towards us. Shadow immediately scuttled behind my legs, where she felt safe! I put on a brave face and tried hard not to panic.

Fortunately (for all of us), the Rottweiler turned out to be a very gentle dog who only wanted to make 'friends'.

Photo 5—Shadow with her first 'football'

Chapter 46
Samson

Early one morning, on my way to the kitchen, my eye was caught by a strange object on the window sill. Switching on the light, I was surprised to see a large cat. Walking around to the front of the house, I gently edged towards it.

Noting he was a male and aware that tomcats can be aggressive, I began by gently rubbing his neck, which he appeared to enjoy. Eventually, he jumped down from the sill and began circling my legs. Wondering if he was hungry, I went to the kitchen and filled a dish with some cat-food. I put the bowl on the ground and the contents soon disappeared.

The cat followed me round to the patio and curled up in the shade of our umbrella, quickly falling sound asleep.

A few minutes later, Shadow and Tinkerbelle ambled into the kitchen. I wondered what they would make of the new arrival. (I was also concerned about John's reaction.)

Our own pets were eager for breakfast and totally ignored our 'guest'. Shadow was the first to show interest and edged towards the interloper. Deciding to let the pets—and John—come to terms with the newcomer, I laid the table for breakfast then went about my morning chores.

Later, I noticed that the cat's collar was extremely tight, so I put the boy on my lap and, with John's help, managed to snip off his 'torment'. The cat sighed with relief, jumped down and went back under the table to resume his siesta. I then spotted rain-clouds on the horizon and put a cushion on a chair in the sitting room. The cat decided this was a much better place to snooze than lying on the patio and settled down for another sleep.

There was no information on Samson's collar. We had hoped that the owner might have etched on his address or telephone number. Our main concern was that someone was pacing the streets looking for their cat, so we left photos of Samson with the local vet and gave copies to both supermarkets.

Thinking about a suitable name for him, I came up with 'Samson'. Although a bit thin, probably through lack of nourishment, he was a large cat.

Photo 6: Samson

Chapter 47
Samson and Shadow

I was concerned about Shadow and Tinkerbelle's reaction to the new addition to the family. However, shortly after Samson's arrival, I saw him pushing his way into Shadow's kennel and squashing up beside her. This was a bit strange. However, as they were beginning to bond, we needed to get Samson checked by a vet as soon as possible. Other than a few ticks, the vet said he was in good shape, in spite of his recent neglect. He wondered if his owner had died, or maybe he decided to look for a new home? Samson appeared remarkably healthy—his only requirement was a proper diet. The vet took away the ticks and also prescribed some powder to clear some mites. He then wished us luck with our 'stowaway'.

On sunny days, Shadow and Samson often curled up on a small trampoline lying on the patio. I was happy that Shadow had found a friend but really concerned about Tinkerbelle—Samson constantly bullied her. This was upsetting in itself, but then he began biting John, who became very anti-Samson. Perhaps the cat had been badly treated by a man and would only trust females?

No one came forward and admitted ownership of the cat so we had no option but to keep him. After obtaining his pet documents, Samson was now legally ours. Shadow was delighted that Samson was staying but John and Tinkerbelle were not particularly happy.

I took great care of Samson, grooming and playing with him every day. He appeared to enjoy my undivided attention and purred noisily while I was brushing him. His favourite game was chasing after a piece of string, constantly trying to catch the cord and snatch it away. (Maybe his former owner had played this game with him?)

He also loved chasing birds. Fortunately, as he was a big cat, he was not agile enough to catch any. Another favourite activity was to wander through the wooded area, searching for voles.

Although Samson was a bit of a rogue, I could not help loving him. Most visitors thought he was 'adorable'—he always managed to worm his way into any heart. Magic seemed to flow from his emerald eyes!

Chapter 48
Pastures New

The next plan was to sell our house in France. Although we loved the villa and its surroundings, we knew it would be expensive to upgrade the whole property. We concluded the best option was to try to find a buyer now (as the house was still in good condition) and search for a new home in the UK. When we moved, we would certainly miss our British and French friends. However, rising inflation had already forced several of our compatriots to leave France.

Later, we considered moving to Spain. We always enjoyed our trips to the Costa del Sol, where we stayed with British friends, who had bought a second-home near Alicante. Their villa was situated in a lovely enclave which included a swimming pool and golf course—plus, the Mediterranean Sea could just be spotted in the distance. We looked at various houses near their property, and further afield, on the internet. However, it was difficult to make an offer on a house without seeing it first.

The next time our friends stopped off for a few days, while én route to Spain, they told us they had decided to sell their Spanish villa as they had various other projects which they needed to finance.

When they left, we discussed all our options and decided to ask them whether we could buy their villa. We phoned and made an offer—which they kindly accepted. As we were due to visit them at Christmas, we agreed this would be a good time to discuss all the formalities.

The next step was to learn Spanish. During our various trips to Alicante, we knew it was important to have at least some knowledge of the local language. After some research, we found a French professor, who agreed to give us lessons at home.

This was great news. Most of the time, we would be able to keep a watchful eye on our three little charges. Occasionally, we all went for a walk round St Maixent, the professor telling us the Spanish names for trees, churches and the various shops we passed.

During a 'home' lesson, the tutor glanced out the window and was surprised to see Shadow and Samson curled up on a trampoline on the patio. He remarked that a dog and a new cat bonding was very 'unusual'.

I explained it was their own decision to team up.

Chapter 49
Hedgehogs

Every dry day, I liked to have a walk around the garden, checking on my flowers and hanging baskets. One morning, I came across two tiny hedgehogs. They looked tired and stressed. Perhaps their mother had abandoned them or had been scared away by a snake or fox? I suspected the babies needed urgent nourishment as they were probably very dehydrated.

First, I ensured the cats and Shadow could not get out of the house. To make the hedgehogs more comfortable, I gently placed them on a cushion near the front door. Next I woke John and asked him to do some research on the internet to discover what to feed baby hedgehogs. Being used to my strange behaviour, he readily complied, and discovered that the best way to rehydrate them was to feed the babies with diluted milk.

After a frantic search for a suitable bottle, I sat on the patio with both hedgehogs on my lap, gently enticing them to suckle some milk. After what seemed an age, eventually they began to respond and between them finished every drop. A few minutes later, they nestled amongst the folds of my dress, falling sound asleep.

Meanwhile, John was building a robust shelter where they could cosy up together. He took a long time building their den. He particularly wanted to ensure their new home would be robust enough to protect the little ones from our pets.

Thinking about what to call the hedgehogs, I decided on Tammy and Toby.

It was essential to bottle-feed them three or four times a day, which I did willingly. Later, I introduced them to cat-food and meal-worms.

Every day, I encouraged them to go for a little walk. However, they seemed to prefer sitting on my shoes—like little ornaments. One morning, I 'walked' them around the whole meadow to acquaint them with their new domain. I was concerned they might get spooked if they went for a wander on their own.

One morning, during our Spanish lesson, I glanced out the window, and spotted Tammy and Toby scuttling under the teacher's car, probably looking for a cool place to sleep. When the professor wanted to leave, I lay on the gravel, trying to coax the babies from their shady 'den'.

Eventually, they came scuttling towards me and sat by my shoes, probably thinking they were going for another walk. Our teacher was speechless. He had never seen young hedgehogs responding to their names and was astonished to see them waiting patiently by my feet. I explained they were expecting a little tour of the garden. The professor was now totally bemused.

Six months later, the hedgehogs disappeared. Although sad to lose them, I presumed they were now old enough to look after themselves and tearfully wished them, 'Bon Voyage'.

Photo 7: Toby—one of the baby hedgehogs

Chapter 50
Wrens

And then there were the wrens! I noticed they were starting to build a nest in one of our hanging baskets on the patio and had visions of Tinkerbelle and Samson waiting for a hatchling to tumble out.

Looking through my bird book, I learned that male wrens always build around five or six nests (called troglodytes as they look like caves). The male would then take his partner on a tour of the garden so she could pick the one that suited all her needs. Surely, this would mean that the female would have many other 'homes' to inspect if I took away the patio nest?

Rather reluctantly, I took down the hanging basket (brim full of crushed pansies) and began to break up the nest. While I was doing this, I got a ticking-off from the male wren, who dive-bombed my head, trying to halt my destruction of a 'potential' home for his babies.

I explained I was doing this because I did not want any little ones to tumble out the nest and be pounced on by our two little terrors. My chatter did not convince him. He continued flying around, shouting out the wren-equivalent of what sounded like rather rude words! Four weeks later, I went into the shed to collect a bottle of flower-food. I almost jumped for joy. There was a beautiful wren's nest, right in the middle of an old hose pipe (which we had hung up on a nail). The nest was ornately decorated with a selection of leaves and flower petals. Fortunately, the shed lacked a door, so there was no risk of any birds being accidentally locked in.

One day, I tiptoed into the shed to collect a hoe. The baby wrens had now hatched and the slight noise I made woke them up. Five little heads peeped out the nest, beaks wide open, awaiting food. I slid away as quietly as possible.

From a safe distance, hiding behind a large bush, I waited with bated breath, hoping to see Mum and Dad flying back to the shed. I crossed all my fingers, praying I had not frightened away their parents. If the chicks had been abandoned, it would be all my fault.

After what seemed like hours, I finally saw Mum and Dad returning, their beaks brimming with tiny worms. I sighed with relief, ecstatic to know that the little ones were going to be fed.

I would certainly not be going near the shed for several weeks—gardening could wait!

Chapter 51
Training Lessons

Later that year, we heard about a dressage group and decided to enrol Shadow for training. We particularly wanted to stop her jumping up at us (or our guests), as well as train her to walk to heel. Shadow would also have the chance to socialise with other dogs. Apart from the odd excursion into town, where she occasionally met another dog, she had never made a 'doggy' friend.

Shadow's training classes took place every Sunday in Pamproux—a few miles from our home. During our first session, she 'jumped up' on the head trainer and was given a harsh lesson. The French way of teaching a dog to stop this behaviour is to knee the animal in the chest, totally winding the poor thing. We were astounded. Rather reluctantly, I have to admit that Shadow never did this again.

Shadow integrated well and appeared to enjoy her lessons. Unfortunately, a large black dog began to bully her. He constantly snapped at Shadow's face and tried to roll her over. The trainers decided to put Shadow and her protagonist into separate groups. However, this dog took every opportunity to attack Shadow. The owner appeared to have no control over his animal's behaviour. Eventually, Shadow began to stand up to her tormentor and would give him the occasional nip.

Training was intense and relentless. At the end of every session, we were told to take our pets for a walk around the village. This seemed to calm down any restless animals. It was good for us too, as we also needed some relaxation.

During our third lesson, I was disillusioned when I overheard two senior trainers chatting and, not realising I understood quite a lot of French, believed I would be unable to comprehend their conversation.

They said it was 'un cauchemar' (a nightmare) when both owners came to training together.

I was mortified. As I cannot drive, John would need to take Shadow to dog training by himself. This was a great pity as I looked forward to our lessons. However, perhaps John and Shadow going to training together might strengthen their bonding.

At the end of the course, Shadow received top marks for obedience. The really good news was that John and Shadow now had total trust in each other. This bond lasted a lifetime.

Chapter 52
Cats

Later in the year, we began making preparations for our 'Christmas' visit to Spain. However, there was one big problem to be resolved—which cat should we take? As Tinkerbelle and Samson still hated one another, it would be a nightmare to take both of them.

Strategically, it would not have been possible to take both cats anyway. Our car was not large enough for two cat boxes, a fast-growing dog, plus our own luggage.

We were still very concerned about Tinkerbelle. She was bullied every day by Samson. He constantly stole her food and, on one occasion, rolled her down the inclined drive towards the road.

Should we take Shadow and Samson who had bonded and find a pet-carer for Tinkerbelle? Or take Shadow and Tinkerbelle who had yet to bond and hope for the best? We were in a quandary. It was now only two weeks till our proposed departure date.

Then a miracle happened. Shadow and Tinkerbelle began to cosy up—first they snuggled up together on the sofa. Later that week, I found them curled up on our bed.

The decision about which cat to take was now easy.

We managed to find Samson an excellent cattery and had the owner's assurance that she would take very good care of him—just as a mother would!

I was on the point of saying that Samson would probably rule the roost, as well as bully all the other cats, but bit my tongue and hoped for the best.

Photo 8: Shadow and Tinkerbelle cosying up

Chapter 53
To Spain

We decided to drive to Alicante in one spurt, rather than spending a night somewhere én route. We thought this would be less stressful for the pets. Previously, when we travelled to Spain, it was only Tinkerbelle we had to worry about. She was content to remain in our bedroom, while we dined in the hotel restaurant. We had no idea how Shadow and Tinkerbelle would react if they were left alone in a strange room—this could be a recipe for disaster. John emphasised he was confident he could manage sixteen hours of driving.

All packed up, the car brimming with our luggage, as well as the all the animal bedding, we were ready to set off on our long journey. Soon after our arrival, our friends were going back to the UK for Christmas, so we would be left to our own devices during the Yuletide season. Although our car was packed solid with our luggage plus the animals' paraphernalia, I managed to find a tiny space for various Yuletide decorations, plus a small musical tree, to make their villa more festive!

Shadow soon curled up on the backseat of the car and quickly fell asleep. Tinkerbelle was already snoozing contentedly in her cat-box. All was calm as we set off for Spain.

The first couple of hours passed quickly. However, when we neared the border, Shadow sat up, put her head on my shoulder, then began to whine and cry. I assumed she wanted to have a pee so we pulled into the first lay-by. Shadow did not want to 'go' and just wandered about. We piled back into the car and, within minutes, she was sound asleep. John contemplated on what may have been the cause of Shadow's agitation. He remembered that the motorway exit (which we passed when Shadow began agitating) was opposite the junction to the Dordogne. It was now over six months since we had purchased Shadow. Was it possible that she could associate a junction on the other side of the motorway with the woes of her early days?

He also said that dogs had an innate sense of distance. Perhaps her instincts kicked in and she was acutely aware we were near the place where she had endured so much suffering? (This might also explain why she constantly whined when we drove from our home into town—she may have thought we were returning her to the puppy farm.)

The terrors she suffered at the police station, plus all the bullying she endured, could last a lifetime. Our only hope was that time, patience and understanding would help her forget these dark days.

Chapter 54
Benidorm

We arrived at the villa in a state of exhaustion. After letting Tinkerbelle out of her cat-box, so she could go off for a wander in the garden, we fed Shadow. As soon as she finished her meal, she fell sound asleep on the sofa. It was now time for a glass of 'bubbly'!

When Tinkerbelle returned from her rambles, she ate a whole tin of food, then curled up on her 'preferred' chair. She also dropped into a deep sleep.

The next day, we visited Benidorm. There is an extensive local market in the centre of town, where you can also purchase real leather goods at a very reasonable price. The main drawback was the various thieves wandering around—you always had to be on the alert.

A 'potential' mugger did bump into me and tried to push me to the ground. Fortunately, John was nearby and came to my rescue. Although a bit shaken, I pushed any dark thoughts to the back of my mind.

After purchasing some lovely gloves and various knickknacks, we all went for a stroll along the esplanade.

The beach in Benidorm stretches as far as the distant headland. A long walk was just what we needed to unravel the backache and knots from our long journey.

The Mediterranean Sea stirred up a gentle breeze which everyone happily embraced. Shadow thoroughly enjoyed sprinting along the beach and had great fun jumping over the waves. While we were having lunch, she fell sound asleep, curled up under our table.

Most evenings, there is a superb show at the Benidorm Palace—plus a gourmet meal included in your entrance ticket. (The meal you have chosen is brought to your table during the first interval.) Before going home, we were lucky to make a booking for the following evening as this was a spectacle not to be missed.

Chapter 55
Animal Sanctuary

When we were in Spain, we always visited Noah's Ark, an animal sanctuary in the mountains, near the Castle of Guadalest. Seran owns the sanctuary and cares for a multitude of animals, including a cross-eyed jaguar, a lynx with rickets, a tiger with spina bifida and a panther with leukaemia. All of those animals have been rescued either from drug-smugglers or circuses.

Some animals get extra-special treatment. A local Spaniard stupidly failed to realise that a fully grown lion is terrified when his only accommodation is a cage in a dark garage. This poor lion is petrified by sunlight. Seran told us that they were slowly introducing him to the joys of daylight.

The sanctuary also cares for around thirty hyper gorillas. These poor gorillas were brain-damaged by people doing a gamut of experimental tests on them (for whatever reason, no one knew). The gorillas are kept in an enormous enclosure, kitted out with swings and ropes. These playthings keep them amused and take their minds off their previous torture. The noise of their joyous screams reverberate throughout the park.

During this particular visit, we spotted a dog with no back legs. Strapped around his waist was a special hand-made trolley. Now, he can amble around with surprising ease. This young Alsatian was very relaxed, full of fun, and appeared to be enjoying life.

The Alsatian trundled over to us, looking for some petting. We all hugged the poor animal, then indulged him with lots of doggy treats. One of the sanctuary staff was keeping watch. Ten minutes later, the keeper came over—it was time for the dog's mid-day meal.

Sadly, we discovered a poor leopard who was suffering with leukaemia. The keeper told us he was recovering and would soon be repatriated with the other leopards. Our hearts went out to him and we wished him a speedy recovery. I even blew him a kiss. He raised an eye, appearing to give me a wink!

I particularly loved going to see the birds. My favourite was a toucan, who always greeted me with glee. He knew I would give his neck a tickle and indulge him with some of his favourite treats.

An adorable Chinese Chow dog, called 'Wrinkles', was the centre's pet. He also loved having lots of attention and was treated royally by the staff. He sat beautifully still while I took his photograph.

There were hundreds of animals to feed and look after. Over the past few years, when we visited the centre, we always made a large donation to their charity.

.

Photo 9: Wrinkles

Chapter 56
The Man in Black

The morning before our friends left for the UK, we all went for a walk around the village. It was a good day for a stroll as the temperature was beginning to drop. On the way back to the villa, we stopped at a local cafe for some refreshments. We were just on the brink of leaving when the owner of a nearby restaurant passed by the cafe. Our friends waved and beckoned him to join us. Pulling up a chair, he sat down for a chat. Shadow was lying under the table, having a little snooze. However, when the 'stranger' sat down, she woke up and started to bark, then began snarling and howling. I tried everything to keep her calm, repeatedly telling her there was nothing to fear. Then Shadow began to growl. We decided it would be best if we left the cafe immediately.

However, the restaurant owner decided to leave, as he believed his presence had been the trigger for Shadow's behaviour. Our friends left with him. We ordered more coffee while we searched our brains for an explanation. Shadow was now curled up under the table, snoring contentedly.

Pondering on what had just happened, I wondered if his dark leather jacket and trousers and the fact that he was jostling a bunch of keys (having just locked up his restaurant) may have reminded Shadow of her time in the police station. Whatever the reason, it was obvious that another dark memory had risen to the surface and Shadow was in mortal terror of being abducted by the 'Man in Black'.

We finished our coffee and left the cafe at the same time as two men, the elder of whom was a bit frail. His companion told us his friend had dementia and he was his carer. Shadow edged closer to them and, just as they asked if she was a friendly dog, Shadow jumped up and kissed the older man on the cheek. The two chaps began laughing at such exuberance.

So happy that she was not being taken away, Shadow began bouncing up and down, then 'danced' all the way back to the villa. The joy she exuded brought tears to my eyes. It was dreadful that she even thought we would send her back to the place where she had suffered so much torment. Many unhappy memories were still engrained in her soul and, sadly, they would probably last for many years.

During the journey back to France, Shadow slept soundly. She made no murmur as we passed the same motorway junction that had caused her so much distress on the way to Spain.

Shadow knew she was on her way home!

Part VI
Wales

Chapter 57
Leaving France

Although our house in France had been on the market for two years, we had no serious bidders. We now needed to up the ante and try to sell quickly. House prices in Spain were escalating and, with those in France now going through the floor, we could no longer afford to buy our friends' villa. We apologised profusely and they were kind enough to appreciate our dilemma. (Fortunately, they sold their house a few months later.)

In 2010, a couple showed interest in buying our home and made an offer—which we happily accepted. Now we needed to track down a temporary residence, preferably in the UK. (By law, we knew it was necessary to rent somewhere for a year before you could buy a house.) We began sourcing places for rent on the internet. This proved a nightmare task. It was impossible to know which house would be suitable for our needs and those of the pets.

Later, we decided to concentrate on finding a property in Wales. During our time abroad, we enjoyed spending part of our leave touring the Welsh countryside, as well as having bracing walks by the sea.

Luckily, John's brother and his wife (who lived in Wales), agreed to have a look at two possible places we tracked down. As it was two days before they left for their holiday house in France, this was a very generous gesture.

They visited both places and rejected our first choice for various reasons. However, they approved of our second option—a bungalow, in the Lampeter area, situated next to the owner's farmhouse.

We immediately contacted the farmer, who agreed to let us rent the property and we, in turn, promised to send him all the relevant references.

Now began the preparations to leave France. Samson was already happily ensconced with his new owners so we could concentrate on tackling the paperwork involved in getting Shadow and Tinkerbelle into the UK.

It was a difficult time—not helped by the boiler blowing up two months before our planned departure date. Also, by law, before you could sell your house, an electrician needed to check the wiring. During this procedure, a major fault was located. Amazingly, he discovered that all the safety circuits had been disconnected.

I squirmed with horror. When defrosting the fridge-freezer, water often sloshed across the floor. I could easily have been electrocuted! The electrician reconnected the circuits, then checked all the wiring in the rest of the house. (We gave him a large tip for all the extra work. In return, he said we could call him anytime if any other problems surfaced.)

After our heavy baggage had been collected, we cleaned the whole villa and firmed up our departure plans.

Chapter 58
Crossing the Channel

Shadow and Tinkerbelle's adventures began with the drive to Calais where we had reserved a night in a hotel. When we arrived, we fed Tinkerbelle and left her sleeping on a blanket.

We took a somewhat distressed Shadow down to the hotel lounge. Not surprisingly, all the upheaval of packing had unsettled her. She seemed very confused and concerned. Looking at me strangely, she appeared to be asking, 'What's happening now, Mummy?'

In the lounge, she began to calm down and ate all our predinner snacks. Shadow soon fell asleep, curled up on the carpet, now aware she was coming with us—one of her major worries had been allayed. When we were settled in the bungalow, I was confident her joie de vivre would bounce back.

The following morning, we boarded the ferry and sailed across the English Channel to Dover. During the voyage, we were given carte blanche to check on the pets. Tinkerbelle was curled up in her cat-cage, sound asleep. Thankfully, Shadow was lying alongside, snoring contentedly. We returned to the upper deck to enjoy some coffee, trying to ignore the pounding waves crashing against the ship.

As soon as we disembarked, we drove along the motorway until we found a suitable place for a picnic. Eventually, we discovered a car park with a large wood nearby. We took Shadow for a long walk through the woods and, as this area was well away from the road, we could unleash her for a scamper. (Tinkerbelle was still sound asleep, snuggled up in her cat-box.)

The bad news was that Shadow and Tinkerbelle would have to be boarded for two days while we moved into our new abode. We were acutely distressed by this and aware that Shadow would be particularly miserable. However, until all the furniture and boxes had been unpacked, we knew the constant upheaval would have been even more unsettling for the pets.

Chapter 59
Lampeter

When we had settled the pets into their respective kennels, we headed for our temporary home on the outskirts of Lampeter. Our route took us along various twisty roads with a scenic backdrop of hills. On the main road, we noticed a removal van in the distance. Maybe our baggage was arriving earlier than expected?

We had just introduced ourselves to our landlord and his wife when a man appeared on the drive. He said his van, presumably carrying our baggage, had got stuck halfway up the lane. A curved stone wall would not allow for any manoeuvring. The farmer said he had a solution. He attached a trailer to his 4x4, then helped John transfer our baggage onto his own transport. This welcoming gesture set the tone for an excellent rapport.

Later that day, the fridge-freezer and washing machine (ordered while in France) also arrived. The following day, we did a mega shop and finished unpacking. The next morning, we went to collect our pets. We were so excited about seeing them and introducing them to their new home.

The bungalow was surrounded by fields, swarming with sheep, forests and a nearby river. We were confident that

Shadow and Tinkerbelle were really going to enjoy their first taste of Welsh country life.

We collected Tinkerbelle first and, after smothering her with kisses (which she hated), put her in the cat-box, then drove to the kennels to collect Shadow. The lady in charge of the dogs said she was quite concerned as Shadow had refused to eat. I immediately knew what had happened.

'When she was given food, did you tell the person feeding her to count to three and say 'Okay'?'

Apparently, the people in charge had forgotten my instructions and Shadow would never eat without permission. I started this when Shadow was a puppy as she used to charge at her food and quickly gobble it down. I managed to curtail such behaviour by making her sit in front of her bowl and counting to ten (later reduced to three) then said 'Okay'. Shadow quickly got the message and would only eat when I said the' magic' word. Thank goodness, we were only separated for two days. The woman at the kennels said she had tried phoning us but mobile phone reception in Ceredigion and the surrounding area was very spasmodic.

We were a bit sceptical but, as the damage had been done, there was no point in further investigation.

Chapter 60
Settling In

Our first task was to introduce the pets to their 'temporary' home. While I prepared lunch, John took the pets for a long walk.

As she did with Blondi, when a walk was on offer, Tinkerbelle could now safely accompany Shadow. This would be the first time Shadow and Tinkerbelle could walk together along a country lane. (They couldn't do this in France. The road alongside our villa was the 'main' route into town and there were no verges or bushes alongside, where Tinkerbelle could hide from the traffic.)

Shadow was somewhat bemused by the cat trotting alongside her, finally accepting this was 'normal' Tinkerbelle behaviour. I watched from the conservatory as they wandered through the nearest field, heading towards a small river. Shadow would no doubt want a paddle—her attachment to water had never waned.

Shadow quickly adapted to her new environment and soon made friends with one of the working sheepdogs, a small collie named Spot. Later, he became known as 'Spot the Ball' as he preferred playing 'fetch' with Shadow, rather than herding sheep!

When the dogs were having games in the meadow, Shadow would sit and wait until Spot brought the ball back to John so the game could continue.

When the farmer saw this happening, he began laughing and said that Spot was now Shadow's 'manservant'.

Chapter 61
Farm Life

Shadow never chased sheep and was only concerned if one animal was standing by itself, away from the flock. She then walked slowly towards the sheep or lamb and nudged it gently back towards the herd. Once the farmer had got the measure of Shadow, she was even allowed to help with rounding up the sheep. Our dog was in her element and really enjoyed being part of the 'team'.

The farmer told us he was really concerned about Tinkerbelle. As she was a small cat, he was worried Tinkerbelle would be terrified by his three large sheepdogs. We were quick to assure him that it was unlikely Tinkerbelle would be scared as she had, on several occasions, chased away any dog that came within her radar.

The first time our tenacious cat ventured into the farmyard, strutting along, head held high, all the big dogs dived into the barn to seek refuge.

Later that day, the farmer told us that he had witnessed this spectacle, totally astounded that such a small cat could terrorise his dogs. He was now sure that Tinkerbelle could look after herself.

Spot, on the other hand, was a bit more adventurous and would occasionally nudge open our conservatory door to see if Shadow wanted a game of ball. If Tinkerbelle was sleeping on top of the chest, her eyes would suddenly open wide. Spot would get a sharp flick of her paw which would send him scurrying headlong into the nearest field.

Life on the farm was a great adventure. We loved our country walks and excursions to various beaches—most situated within an hour's driving distance. On sunny days, we went exploring, often driving to Newquay—where Shadow could paddle in the sea—or going for long walks through nearby nature reserves. There were also numerous paths wending their way through the woods, all criss-crossed by tumbling streams and surrounded by a multitude of different plants.

Shadow was now back on track. Thankfully, all her agitation and fear when we were leaving France had totally dissipated.

Chapter 62
Spot Saves the Day

When John was at work, I often took Shadow and Spot for a walk through the fields. One afternoon, when the dogs were chasing each other through the meadows, I went for a wander ending up near a ditch, running alongside a hedge. Stupidly, I leant forward and peered into the stream, slipped on the grass, ending five feet down in claggy mud.

Unable to find anything to help pull me out of the mire, I stood on tiptoe and spotted Shadow and Spot in the distance. I tried calling them to no avail.

Shadow was happily exploring beneath the hedges, no doubt looking for voles, and turned a deaf ear to my pleas for help. However, Spot sensed I was having a problem and hared across the field. He peered into the ditch, lowered his head, and stared avidly into my eyes. I wondered what he wanted me to do.

Spot did not budge but kept gazing at me. Finally, I realised his intention. I raised my arms, wrapping them around his strong neck. Bracing himself, Spot began to back away, gradually pulling me out of the mire. Although Spot was very strong, our progress was pitifully slow.

Nearing the top, I spied a bunch of tufted grass along the edge of the ditch and managed to grab a handful. Now I could take some of the strain off Spot. Eventually, still holding onto Spot, I was able to clamber out from the ditch, then collapsed on the ground.

Shadow came running over, looking somewhat bemused, mainly because I was covered in mud and bleeding from various scratches. Spot was also stretched out on the grass, recovering from his heroic effort. I waited for the pounding in my heart to subside. When I felt able to sit up, I gave both dogs a big cuddle.

Shadow was very confused and stared fixedly at my general disarray. However, this did not stop her nudging Spot so they could have another run through the fields. Poor Spot—no peace for this brave dog.

Slowly, I began walking home. When Shadow and Spot caught up with me, we made our way back to the bungalow. I gave both dogs a handful of treats, then heard the farmer calling Spot so he raced off to do his sheep-herding duty.

I sat on the chest in the conservatory with Tinkerbelle curled up beside me, Shadow asleep at my feet.

I really needed a bath and the resulting soak began to soothe the various aches and pains.

Chapter 63
Shadow Learning English

We were eager to continue Shadow's training and made an appointment to meet the person who ran the local group. Sally tested Shadow's responses to 'Sit', 'Down', 'Stay' and then checked her agility by running round the field, while holding her leash.

The main problem was the language barrier. All Shadow's training had taken place in France and, as I always spoke to her in French, she rarely responded to English commands.

Nevertheless, she was accepted into the group and thoroughly enjoyed meeting all the other dogs, relearning how to jump over hurdles and wind through upright sticks. Gradually, she began to make some progress with her 'new' language.

During one lesson, the trainer pointed out that although Shadow was more than three-quarters labrador, she also had a touch of pointer in her. We had often wondered why Shadow did not have a typical labrador face.

The pointer part was now much more apparent—around the base of her back legs, there were several white hairs, while the rest of her coat was totally black. She also had white eyelashes which was very unusual.

During lambing season, we adored watching the little ones suckling the ewes' milk, furiously wagging their tiny tails as they imbibed their nourishment. Another spectacle were the Charlie C130s flying through the valley. Sadly, the noise made by their vast engines was ear-splitting and always terrorised poor Tinkerbelle.

Chapter 64
A Village in West Wales

When our lease was drawing to an end, we began looking for a permanent home in Wales. We were, of course, keenly aware that Shadow and Spot would be deeply unhappy to be separated.

When Shadow had her third birthday, we bought her a proper football, which became her greatest treasure.

Photo 10: Shadow (aged 3) with her new football

As the weeks went by, and with no success in finding a new home, we became quite desperate. It was only a few weeks till our lease came to an end. We had toured most of Wales, visiting a multitude of places up for sale. None came anywhere near our 'dream home'.

One morning, we had a call from John's sister-in-law. She knew the type of house we were searching for and thought she had found somewhere that ticked all our boxes. Emphasising that this house would soon be snapped up, she said it was imperative to view the property immediately and arrange an appointment with a solicitor.

We were totally exhausted with all the trips we had made and did not relish another long journey but what if she was right and we lost the chance of our ideal home? We arranged a viewing the next day and were so glad we did.

As we were driving through the village, on the way to the house, we were delighted to note that it had a duck pond and a local shop too. All the residences were built in different architectural styles and various trees embellished their gardens. Plus, the backdrop of hills gave the impression of real 'country-living'.

Chapter 65
New Home

We were made welcome by the current owner and were delighted to see there were two bedrooms, sitting and dining area, plus a conservatory, kitchen (with utility room) and a study. From the kitchen window, we could see a large garden which was separated from another area by a gated fence.

We ventured into the garden. There was a large patio outside the back door and a gravel path leading towards the fenced-off area. We decided to explore this 'wild' part of the garden.

It was a delight to see an abundance of wildflowers sprinkled amongst the many trees. At the foot of a steep incline, we could see a rocky stream tumbling over various rocks. I was also totally enthralled by the number of birds flitting around. Bird-watching is my favourite hobby and, if the deal went through, I would be in my element feeding and tending to my avian friends.

The owner told us there was one oak and three ash trees growing in the 'wild area' and that the stream weaved its way towards another tributary. The two streams then joined forces and headed to the duck pond.

If the house deal went through, the owner explained that responsibility for the maintenance of the preserved oak and ash trees would lie in our court (as dictated by the council). These trees would need pollarding every four or five years. A factor we had not anticipated but were happy this was the only extra expense.

The lady of the house was delighted when we said we would be making an offer and was even more pleased when we offered to buy any furniture up for sale. She said this was great news as she was anticipating having to sell most of her heavy goods through eBay.

As we had sold all our furniture prior to leaving France, happily we could now replace almost everything we needed.

Chapter 66
Leaving Lampeter

Before we headed back to Margam, we did a tour of the surrounding area and discovered that the location of the village was very close to the Bristol Channel. When we arrived at the sea-front, we were hugely impressed by the vastness of the long beach at Aberavon. This would be an ideal place to let Shadow run free. She could also play 'fetch', have a paddle and meet up with other dogs.

On the way back to Lampeter, I kept all my fingers crossed, praying there would be no hiccups to the deal being finalised. After the usual protracted negotiations, and a few tense moments when everything seemed to be going amiss, we finally purchased our new home.

We would miss Lampeter very much and, to thank everyone for their hospitality and kindness, we organised a leaving party at the local inn. In return, we received so many parting gifts. Everyone said how much they would miss Shadow, and the farmer and his wife presented us with a lookalike furry toy that was a replica of Spot.

The next morning, we packed the last of our belongings. The furniture and beds had already been collected by a removal company and would be delivered to our new home the next day.

Spot came to see us while we were saying our goodbyes. Against his better nature, he allowed me to give him a big cuddle. Then Spot went over to Shadow and touched her nose. It was heart-breaking watching the dogs saying goodbye.

John told Spot he would bring Shadow back to Cellan for a visit. He kept his promise later that year.

Chapter 67
Shadow Makes a New Friend

As soon as we moved into our new home, we set about preparing for the arrival of our baggage. Tinkerbelle was eager to explore the garden and set off to investigate her new surroundings. She had never accepted that a cat should be kept indoors for three weeks before being let out. (When we first arrived in Brussels in 2003, she had promptly ignored that particular rule.)

After lunch, John took Shadow for a walk and met up with a lady, who was walking her dog in a nearby field. Her pet was a Lurcher, called Lizzie. Sadly, we thought it unlikely that two females would bond.

It turned out that Shadow and Lizzie's friendship would last a lifetime. When John went to collect his morning paper, he would often bump into Lizzie and her mum near the local shop. After a few jumps and scampers, the dogs would continue their walk around the village.

As Lizzie's mum sometimes worked full-time, John would often take both pets for a long walk in the afternoon. They usually went to Margam Park as the dogs loved seeing the donkeys. There were lots of other animals around, too—deer, ducks, rabbits, pigs, sheep and goats to name but a few.

Shadow was extremely enamoured of the various lakes and took every opportunity to have a swim, regardless of the weather.

Occasionally, both of us took the dogs for a picnic in the Brecon Beacons. The girls loved chasing each other up steep hills, splashing in the little rivers, and meandering through the bracken. When we arrived home, exhausted by their exertions, the dogs lay side-by-side in our garden snoozing contentedly.

Lizzie always stayed with us when Mum and Dad went overseas to visit family members living in Europe. The dogs never grumbled at each other over food or treats and Shadow even allowed Lizzie to sleep on her favourite bed. It appeared we were meant to come to the village just for Shadow's sake.

Yes, she would really miss Spot but, thankfully, Lizzie would help fill this big gap in her life.

Chapter 68
Shadow and Children

Shadow always came to 'Mummy' when she had a problem which was not easily noticed. She would press her body against my legs, indicating I should run my hands through her coat to search for the cause of her distress. It might be something simple like a tick, which had beaten its way through the various 'barriers', or even a flare-up of her wet eczema. (Sometimes this problem was not apparent—mainly because the inflammation was usually hidden under her collar or covered by the hair on her chest.)

Shadow was always right—there was something that needed attention. As soon as this had been dealt with, Shadow thanked me by licking my hand.

It was the children in the local primary school who spread Shadow's fame far and wide. They were mystified that our dog mainly responded to commands in French. John explained that Shadow was brought up in France and was in the process of learning English. Naturally, this would help Shadow adapt to living in Britain.

This news spread throughout the school—a dog that comprehended French! We rarely saw Tinkerbelle who was always outdoors exploring her new domain, occasionally deigning to come home for dinner. She could also be a real terror and I often had to catch her before she pounced on an unsuspecting bird.

Tinkerbelle would sit stock-still, watching avidly as the birds scrabbled for worms under the silex tree. Suddenly, she would run like wildfire, hoping to snare a poor bird. Fortunately, I was quick off the mark too, and often managed to save any birds coming within her radar.

I decided to attach a little bell to Tinkerbelle's collar, hoping this would alert any birds to a 'cat on the prowl'.

Chapter 69
Jasper

A few months later, there was a new addition to the family. During a visit to a pet shop, I spotted some adorable baby parrots and discovered these were green-cheeked conures. I was overjoyed when one of the conures jumped onto the bars of his cage, wanting to make friends. This tiny bird gently nibbled my finger while I stroked his toes. I was in love. John was shaking his head and mouthing, 'No, no, no!'

Naturally, I ignored all his frantic signalling and asked to see the shop manager. I explained we were just about to leave for Switzerland to visit my nephew and his wife. However, I really wanted to purchase one of the newly-fledged conures.

The manager was very understanding and offered to help, saying she would take this particular parrot home and look after him till we returned. After agreeing a fee, John paid up, knowing he was on a lost cause. The manager asked what I planned to call him. I thought for a moment, then decided on 'Jasper'.

'Why Jasper?' she queried.

'Well, he has such piercing black eyes and has the aura of a bird who will soon be up to all kinds of mischief. Just the kind of pet I will adore!'

The manager smiled, although I noted a hint of sympathy in her eyes.

As soon as we returned from Zurich, we collected Shadow (who had been staying with Lizzie) then went to the shop to fetch our baby parrot. I asked the manager if Jasper had been any trouble.

'None at all. It took him a few days to become accustomed to our dog, but before long he began sitting on Paddy's head. Paddy would then walk Jasper all around the house. I suspect your parrot will be a great companion.'

It was a great relief to learn that Jasper was friendly and tolerated dogs. When we arrived home, we quickly settled him into his cage.

To accustom him to his new environment, my morning routine was to put Jasper on my head, where he nestled into my hair. Then I tended to a few chores.

Window cleaners and our gardener could often be heard chortling if they looked through the conservatory door and spotted me dusting, with a sleepy parrot perched on my head!

Chapter 70
Jasper's Daily Routine

It soon became apparent that Jasper had the makings of a great companion. In the morning, when I removed his cover, he clung onto the bars of his cage, waiting for his morning kiss. I was also convinced he was trying to speak. One morning, I clearly heard him say, 'Yes, Ma'am.'

He was copying John. This was his usual response when I reminded him of certain tasks that needed to be dealt with—something he had picked up from one of my bosses, when I reeled off his daily agenda.

Jasper's vocabulary increased daily. He began calling me 'Mummy' but, for some reason, called John 'Jabby'. His morning routine was to ask for apple and cel (celery). When I was trying to insert his breakfast treats between the bars of his cage, occasionally, a piece fell on the floor. Jasper always screeched, 'Dropped it!'

Jasper always indicated what he wanted by making coughing noises, especially if you forgot to give him his morning toast. His vocabulary increased daily. He said 'Christmas' when something good to eat was offer, and 'Yes, dear' when I was teaching him new words. He also adored nestling in John's palm while they watched rugby together.

During afternoon playtime, he often wanted a bath. His way of bathing was to sit on a little plastic boat under tepid running water. When completely drenched, he rolled around on top of my head—drying himself in my hair—then flew up to the top of the kitchen door to rearrange his feathers.

When he had finished preening, he played with his toys and nibbled at his afternoon snack. Any food not to his taste would be tossed on the floor. His favourite 'dish of the day' was a plate of sugar-cane and chilli. This attraction never waned.

Shadow accepted Jasper although she hated him trying to land on her head—a quick 'woof' and Jasper got the message. As for Tinkerbelle, she would have loved to catch our little lad and once nearly succeeded. Jasper had flown through to the sitting room and was sitting on the top of the sofa, peering at people and cars passing by the house.

A few moments later, Tinkerbelle—who had been asleep upstairs on our bed—suddenly appeared and leapt at Jasper. Fortunately, I was close by and lunged towards Tinkerbelle, grasping her back legs before she caught my boy. He seemed quite unperturbed by this near-miss and casually flew back to his cage.

Jasper also learned to open his cage door so we had to resort to a padlock—then he started swinging around his seed dish so he could escape when he wanted!

No matter what he did, I adored him so much and he reciprocated this love by giving me very gentle 'kisses'.

Photo 11: Jasper at playtime

Chapter 71
Jasper Has a Tantrum

One weekend, a couple of friends came to stay. Dave and Val knew Tinkerbelle very well and had met Shadow in France, during our last visit to Spain. However, this was their first introduction to Jasper. In the afternoon, John took Shadow out for her afternoon walk. Val was in the sitting room watching Wimbledon, with Tinkerbelle asleep on her lap. Closing the conjoined doors, I decided this was a good time to let Jasper free to stretch his wings.

Dave was already in the conservatory, reading a newspaper, and confirmed it would be fine if Jasper came out to 'play'.

While we were reminiscing about our overseas travels, we left Jasper to his own devices. My wee lad seemed quite content. He flew around the room, then launched himself at his snack, totally ignoring our guest.

After about fifteen minutes, Val shouted through the door, saying Tinkerbelle had woken up and was miaowing for food. Leaving Dave alone with Jasper, I went into the utility room and put more cat-food in Tinker's bowl. She quickly demolished the contents, then dashed into the garden.

Now I heard Dave yelling for help. I quickly ran back to the conservatory—horrified to find Jasper biting savagely at Dave's neck!

Quickly catching my little horror, I put him back in his cage, wondering what on earth had brought on this temper tantrum. Jasper had always been happy to stay with his 'minder' when we went on holiday. However, this was the first time he had been left alone, with a stranger, in his 'own' territory. Perhaps this had frightened him—but not half as much as it had terrified Dave, who was now applying a soothing cream to his neck!

The next day, we left the pets to their own devices while we went off to the races at Ffos Las. Before leaving, John put a padlock on Jasper's cage door and taped up his seed and oyster shell dishes to close off his other escape routes. I prayed my menagerie would behave themselves, hoping we would not return to chaos.

Our day at the races went well, in all respects. Lunch was most enjoyable and both Dave and I managed to back some winners, too. A great day, all round.

During the drive home, I convinced myself our house would be in turmoil. Despite my fears, all the pets had behaved impeccably. John took Shadow for a ramble in the park and I let Jasper out for a fly.

Dave and Val wisely decided to sit out on the patio, keeping Tinkerbelle company.

Chapter 72
Lost in the Woods

During the next few months, we thoroughly explored Margam Park, trying to find a good spot to watch the deer. This was difficult, as they often meandered through mountainous areas or hid away in the bracken. One autumn day, John and Shadow came across a sheltered spot in the woods, where a herd of deer had taken up residence.

Later that week, I prepared a picnic lunch and we set off (hopefully) to see the deer. John said it would be safe to take Shadow along too, as this area was surrounded by a plethora of bushes, growing alongside a fenced hedge. Surely, the presence of two spectators and a calm dog would not frighten the deer?

Shortly after finishing lunch, we were delighted to see a herd of deer gathering in the field. Eventually, they came right up to the fence, intent on having a closer look at their admirers—totally unperturbed by the presence of a dog. This was a magical moment. (Sadly, I had forgotten my camera.)

When it was time to go home, I discovered my balance had gone awry. The recurring corn on my toe was now throbbing like crazy. I could barely walk. John said he would take Shadow home, fetch the car, and explained how to get to the main road where he would pick me up. When they left, I began hobbling, aiming for the main road. However, the pain was now so acute that I became disorientated and lost my bearings.

When he was walking across the field, John sensed that Shadow was somewhat distressed. He explained that he was going to take her home, fetch the car, and find Mummy. Shadow cottoned onto these 'magic' words (which she remembered from the games we played in France).

'Find Mummy' meant only one thing to Shadow.

Shadow pulled the lead out of John's hand and took off like a rocket, running full-pelt back towards the wood. There was no way John could catch her, so he raced home to pick up the car. He was concerned Shadow might return to our original picnic area, lose my scent and get lost in the woods (or may even get run-down if she headed onto the road).

At this point, I was struggling on, hoping my instincts were taking me towards the road. Suddenly, I heard a rustling sound behind me. Thinking it might be a fox or badger spurred me to greater efforts. I tried to walk faster. In my panic, I stumbled over a small log, hidden amongst the vegetation, which brought me to my knees. Unable to get back on my feet, I lay down on the bracken, closed my eyes and waited for the pain to ease.

The next thing I knew was the touch of a very wet tongue licking my face. Opening my eyes, I was amazed to see Shadow hovering over me. She bent her head, just as Spot had done in Lampeter during the 'ditch' drama. I reached up and put my arms around her neck. Shadow braced herself and gently pulled me into an upright position, then we cuddled up together.

Feeling more stable, I crawled towards the nearest tree and edged myself upright. Tightly holding Shadow's lead, we both weaved our way slowly through the undergrowth.

Eventually, I heard the noise of traffic. Hopefully, we were now heading in the direction of the main road.

Meanwhile, John was driving slowly back and forth, peering into the wood. At last he spied us. Sighing with relief, he pulled up on the verge and quickly bundled both of us into the car.

As soon as we arrived home, Shadow was rewarded with lots of treats, while I soaked the offending toe in hot, salty water.

The following day, I saw a chiropodist. He explained that the last person who treated me for corns had left a sliver of metal in my toe, which had probably contaminated my blood. He treated the offending toe and also prescribed a strong dose of antibiotics.

Chapter 73
A Visit to the Scottish Isles

My best friend at school and her husband had recently retired to Islay—an island far out in the Atlantic, close to the Isle of Jura. We thought this would be an ideal place for a holiday. Apart from our honeymoon in Arran, we had never visited any other Scottish Isles. Our research revealed that Islay is surrounded by a plethora of sandy beaches. We also noted there was a nature park and an RSPB centre. This sounded a great place for a break—we were sure Shadow would agree too.

We phoned our friends to enquire if we could pay a visit, with Shadow. They were somewhat hesitant about Shadow coming. When I pressed them for a reason, they told me they had undergone a dreadful experience when they met up with another couple in a mainland hotel. The dog who accompanied their friends was totally out of control, barked continuously and ran riot throughout the bar and restaurant.

This nerve-wracking experience explained their reluctance regarding Shadow. I explained that our dog was well-behaved, not aggressive, and always obedient. After a great deal of thought, they decided to give Shadow the benefit of the doubt.

Shadow was now four years old and a well-travelled dog. Even the nightmare drive up to Scotland (queues, pounding rain, long diversions) did not faze her. However, she really enjoyed the ferry trip to Islay and, once we arrived, gazed longingly through the window at the sandy shores and sparkling sea.

We found a parking place close to the shore and let Shadow free. She bounded towards the sea—running like a tornado across the beach. After a quick dip, she clambered over various rocks then leapt onto the highest boulder, raising her head skywards, barking with sheer delight.

It was also great to see so many birds dipping and diving through the fluffy clouds. A real treat was watching the oyster catchers digging for worms in the sand—all totally ignoring the 'strangers on the shore!'

After an hour of meandering along the shore, Shadow once again ran full-pelt across the sand, headed for the sea, then began jumping over the waves. Exhausted but happy, she eventually walked slowly back to the car. A few minutes later, stretched out on her blanket, Shadow dropped into a deep sleep.

During our holiday, Shadow was on her best behaviour. When we first sat down for lunch in our friends' kitchen, they asked if Shadow could go into the sitting room. I looked at Shadow and said in French, 'Would you leave the kitchen, please?'

Shadow obediently went into the sitting room and lay down on her bed. Our hosts could barely believe Shadow had responded to such a gentle command.

When we went out for lunch, Shadow curled up under the table and snoozed till it was time to leave.

She never begged for food but was delighted if a morsel happened to 'drop' on the ground!

Chapter 74
A Fond Farewell

During our stay, we were so fortunate with the weather. The sun shown nearly every day and it was warm enough to paddle in the little coves and bays. The scenery was stupendous. There were masses of wild flowers, birds and butterflies everywhere. We visited a walled garden—brimming with all sorts of trees, flowers and bushes—meandered through an RSPB nature park, and strolled along various sandy beaches, where Shadow could run off any pent-up energy.

Occasionally, we would just lounge in our friends' garden and let the gentle mist and breezes from the Atlantic swirl around us—evoking the image that we were all part of a hazy Chagall painting.

Every morning, John took Shadow to a sheltered cove not far from the house. There she could dive into the water and swim near the seals. None of the seals seemed to mind her presence and Shadow was sensible enough to keep her distance and not distress them.

On our last night, John and I retired early as we needed to rise at 5 am. (The first ferry left at 7.30 am.)

Shadow decided to stay up a little longer.

In the morning, our hosts told us that, before retiring, Shadow had given them 'a paw'—presumably her own way of saying, 'Thank you for having me.'

This touching gesture totally floored them.

When we were packing up the car, Shadow ran back to the house. Our hosts were standing at the front door, ready to wave goodbye. Shadow began nudging their hands, so she could lick their fingers, presumably saying her own farewell.

We strongly believe Shadow was acutely aware of our friends' wariness of dogs and was trying to reassure them that she was in a totally different class.

Chapter 75
Mount Snowdon

Our next holiday was decided by the fact that we had never visited Snowdonia. We tracked down a holiday home near the seaside town of Barmouth, within easy reach of the local train station.

When we arrived, we were delighted by our holiday home which was ideal for all our needs. The surrounding area was criss-crossed by various streams and an abundance of trekking paths. Just right for us and one energetic dog!

The next day, we set off for the railway station. Sadly, we discovered that dogs were not allowed on the train which went to the top of Snowdonia. However, dogs were allowed on the two smaller trains—one went around Lake Padarn and the other train went to Nant Gwernol by the coast.

During the lake trip, I was enchanted to see Mt Snowdon, encircled by fluffy clouds. Shadow was in her element too. She adored trains, having become accustomed to them during various holiday trips through the Scottish Highlands.

Lake Padarn is the sixth deepest lake in Wales and has been home to the Arctic Char since the last Ice Age. The dark, glistening water mirrored the huge mountains towering around the edge of the lake.

At the end of the line, the engine needed to be reversed for the return trip. While this was happening, we were told we could either have a wander in the nearby park or stay on the train and admire the view. I opted to remain in the carriage and take photos of the splendid scenery. John and Shadow headed for the park.

After a few minutes, I glanced through the carriage door, astounded to see Shadow running up and down the platform, checking every compartment. Hearing me calling her, she came bounding towards me. To help Shadow clamber up the steep steps, I had to lean out the door, catch hold of her collar, and ease her into the train. Once aboard, she began licking my hand then sat down by my feet. John was next to appear. He could not believe Shadow had jerked the lead out of his hand and ran off.

Thinking back, I remembered that Shadow seemed to hate us being apart when we went for a ramble in the countryside. When I was tired, I often rested on a log or boulder, while John and Shadow set off for a longer walk. After a few minutes, Shadow would rush back to check I was still where she had left me. If I was at home when they went for a walk, Shadow had no qualms.

Now, it all made sense—she felt Mummy needed protecting when outdoors in the big wide world!

Chapter 76
More Train Fun

The next train went to Nant Gwernol. Rolling through lush, rolling countryside, we headed for the coast. Shadow appeared content to look through the window at the passing scenery.

When we reached the terminus, I bought some refreshments at the buffet bar while John took Shadow for a walk, heading for the sea. However, they had to turn back before reaching the coast—the train was due to depart in ten minutes. Shadow was very glum—swimming was one of her main enjoyments in life.

On the return journey, Shadow quickly fell asleep. When she woke up, she began to fidget and began eyeing up the people in our carriage. (Each section had four seats but there was no central passageway.) Shadow spotted a friendly face in the row behind us and promptly managed to wriggle under the seat to greet this lady. With difficulty, John crawled under the seat too, in an effort to bring Shadow back. Now, our mischievous dog jumped up on the seat behind me. Looking down at John, Shadow seemed somewhat perplexed—why was her master lying on the floor? All the passengers burst into hysterical laughter. (I think they believed this was part of the tour's entertainment.) In the end, a handful of treats decided matters. Seeing the treats, Shadow decided to crawl back under the seat and sat by my feet.

Meanwhile, John was trying to join us and he too began wriggling under the seat. When he eventually stood up, everyone in the carriage clapped.

Thinking the applause was for her, Shadow jumped back on the seat again, acknowledging their appreciation of 'free entertainment' with a quick 'Woof'!

Chapter 77
Shadow at the Dog Show

Later that year, we heard there was a dog show in Margam Park. There were also several competitions in which pets could participate. We decided to take Shadow to see if she remembered her training in France and Lampeter. Running through barrels and weaving between upright sticks were her main forte.

Shadow quickly demonstrated that she had not forgotten her training lessons. However, as she was a bit older now, she could not match the younger dogs' agility and they easily outmanoeuvred her.

The last competition was 'The Best Six Legs'. As it was an extremely hot day, John was wearing shorts so they were granted permission to enter for this event. After several rounds, Shadow and John's only competitor for first place was a gorgeous long-legged lady and her little dog.

They were first to parade around the circuit. Then Shadow and John had their turn—showing the adjudicators their beautifully-crafted legs. The judges huddled together to decide a winner.

I crossed all my fingers and toes that John and Shadow would win and, to my great joy, they were voted 'Best Six Legs'!

We were then obliged to pose for a photo. A professional photographer snapped three grinning faces!

Photo 12: Shadow Wins 'Best Six Legs'

Chapter 78
Shadow's Brush with Death

In general, Shadow was a healthy dog. However, one day, keen to know what was hiding in the grass, she plunged her head into a clump of vegetation and was bitten by a young adder. John believed Shadow must have disturbed mother's nest as he spotted lots of baby adders slithering around.

When they arrived home, I was horrified that Shadow's cheeks were swollen and she was gasping for breath. I quickly rang the vet and was told to take Shadow immediately to their main surgery in Brackla. On arrival, she was hooked up to a drip, which pumped anti-venom medication through her system. The vet warned us there was no guarantee as to whether Shadow would survive this ordeal.

When the phone rang, we were almost too frightened to pick up the receiver in case the news was about Shadow's demise. A nail-biting time, not helped by Tinkerbelle refusing to eat. Was she sick too? I wondered.

A week later, a nurse rang to say Shadow had turned a corner and was on the way to recovery. We could collect her in two days' time.

Time to open the champagne!

When we collected Shadow, we noticed she had lost a lot of weight but was otherwise perky and eager to come home. Even Tinkerbelle gave Shadow a warm welcome. She practically insisted they should cuddle up together on the sofa.

The next major problem occurred when Shadow turned ten and needed an operation to remove a tumour from her underbelly. Luckily, she also overcame this second ordeal.

Shadow touched the vet's hearts many times with her amusing antics. When we arrived at the surgery, she would bounce into the practice and aim straight for the scales. She would sit patiently while her weight was checked, eagerly waiting for her biscuit.

With her lovely brown eyes looking at them so appealingly, Shadow always received an extra handful of treats before she left the practice.

Chapter 79
Tinkerbelle

In 2014, shortly before her twentieth birthday, Tinkerbelle began to lose weight and, despite extra medication and special nutritious food from the vet, her appetite continued to diminish.

Later that week, John and I sat on the patio playing Scrabble—Tinkerbelle asleep on a chair between us. She seemed much calmer now and we hoped she was now responding to her tablets. Regretfully, in my heart, I knew that Tinkerbelle was very ill. Her birthday was due in August. Would she live to see it?

The following morning, I found Tinkerbelle cuddled up against my back, deep in sleep. This was odd—several months ago, she stopped coming upstairs as this seemed to cause her some distress.

As I was preparing breakfast, Tinkerbelle began acting strangely, looking very disorientated. Then she wandered around in a daze, unsuccessfully trying to find her litter box.

John rang the vet and explained Tinkerbelle's distress. He was told to bring her to the surgery at once. As he was dressed, ready for his walk with Shadow, John decided to leave immediately.

Although I knew she would resist being cuddled, I gave Tinkerbelle a huge hug and a big kiss, then gently put her in the cat-box.

After John left, I noticed that Shadow was trembling. Although Shadow did not interact with Tinkerbelle, as she had with Blondi, there was still a deep bond between them. I put my arms around Shadow and held her close till she calmed down. Later, I showered and dressed, praying the news about my darling cat would be better than expected.

John phoned from the surgery. The vet had told him it would be a kindness to put Tinkerbelle to sleep, immediately. Our darling cat was suffering acute pain and, due to her age, there was no medication available that would have any effect.

Reluctantly, we agreed with the vet's diagnosis.

When he arrived home, John was choking back tears. Apparently, when he put Tinkerbelle on the vet's examination table, she seemed aware of what was going on. Lying down, she pressed her head into John's hand. The euthanasia injection took immediate effect and she quickly passed away.

We hugged each other, saying a little prayer for Tinkerbelle. However, we were happy she was now at peace and free from pain. Perhaps she would find her beloved Blondi in heaven? I could just imagine them scampering about together, jumping from cloud to cloud.

While we were talking, Shadow started whining (aware something bad had happened) then she ran into the garden, searching everywhere for Tinkerbelle,

How to tell a pet that her companion has gone forever is not in any textbooks I have read. It was going to take a long time before Shadow accepted that Tinkerbelle would not be coming home.

On one of our walks around the village (a few days after our cat had passed away), we came across a lookalike Tinkerbelle. Shadow stopped dead and began to whine noisily.

The cat did not budge. Looking at us intently, she appeared to be wondering why our dog was in such a state.

We gradually pulled Shadow away, repeatedly telling her that we were not abandoning her companion.

Eventually, Shadow bowed her head, appearing to understand what we were saying.

Chapter 80
Jasper, Where Are You?

Sadly, we lost Jasper in 2020, when he was almost ten years old. We had been on a cruise to the Canary Islands and, as soon as we returned, we collected Jasper from his carers. He was overjoyed to see us and began running through his vast repertoire. I gave him loads of kisses and indulged him with his favourite sugar-cane and chillies.

Later that week, when John returned from his walk with Shadow, he went into the utility room to fetch Shadow some treats. Jasper was sitting on top of the kitchen door—as he did every day—waiting for John to return. I was in the conservatory tidying up Jasper's toys and could hear him prattling away.

John went back outside to give Shadow her treats, failing to notice that Jasper had flown onto his shoulder. (Jasper had never done this before as he usually waited until John had sat down with his tea, then snuggled into his hand.)

When John heard a series of loud chirps, he was horrified to see our wee lad sitting on his shoulder. He began to panic and tried to catch hold of him. This spooked Jasper and he took off, flying in circles under the parasol. John banged on the conservatory window to alert me to the drama. Looking out, I was horrified to see my wee boy flying around the patio. I dashed outside and frantically began calling, 'Jasper, Jasper baby—come to Mummy!'

He circled around my head then, totally disorientated, flew over the conservatory roof, heading towards the garden gate. I kept repeating his name, willing him to land on my head. In mid-flight, he turned around. I was convinced he was coming towards me and stood very still.

However, at the last minute, something spooked him and Jasper flew straight past me, delving into the heart of the village. In spite of my pleas, he did not turn around and was soon out of sight.

I sat for hours on the patio, ringing his favourite bell, calling his name, praying he would come back to Mummy. Meanwhile, John was searching all through the village, telling anyone he met to look out for our little parrot.

The lockdown for COVID in 2020 had recently started, which meant some people were already working from home. Hopefully, with more neighbours around, Jasper had a better chance of being found.

John alerted our neighbours (via Facebook) to look out for Jasper. The following morning, he printed off posters of our boy (promising a reward for the 'finder'), then stuck the leaflets on every lamp post in the village.

Sadly, we never found out what had happened to Jasper. Had he been killed by a buzzard, died alone and frightened, huddled in a tree, or even picked up by someone who decided to keep him?

Jasper is ringed and chipped. If he is taken to any of the lost and found rescue centres, they have instructions to contact us. We live in hope that one day someone will telephone us with the great news that our wee lad has been found safe and well.

Chapter 81
Birds

I consoled myself by overindulging my beloved garden birds. The resident sparrows always made nests in the large bush near the patio. Totally, ignoring my presence, every day they scuttled between my legs, picking up any spilled seed from their food container. Some days, I indulged them with handfuls of mealworms. However, I had to be alert as eagle-eyed starlings are always looking for treats too. If any special food was on offer, they usually muscled in to steal the sparrows' treats.

At nesting time, the youngsters added to the fun and the garden was often ablaze with a plethora of different birds, usually fighting over the various bird food on offer. We also have several bird baths scattered around—a great attraction for all our avian friends.

At the last RSPB Bird Count, we realised we had over thirty different bird species coming to our garden, ranging from giant ravens and sparrow hawks to tiny wrens.

Although we have decal stickers on our conservatory windows, occasionally a bird would fly straight into the glass, often tumbling to the ground. If it was just stunned, I held it upright, while checking its wings and legs for any damage. If there was no apparent injury, I left the bird to recover in its own time.

If the bird's feet were curled in a ball, I needed to hold the bird upright on the patio table, talking soothingly and gently unwinding its toes. When the bird began showing interest and looking around, I placed it under the big hedge beside the patio, where he would be happier and could recover in safety.

One morning, when John was out walking with Shadow, a young dove crash-landed on the patio. My immediate thought was that this poor bird had died. However, I picked him up, holding him against my breast, gently stroking his plumage.

After five long minutes, there was a reaction. The dove slowly opened his eyes, then began struggling. I gently told him it was too soon to try to fly. He needed to rest a little longer. Placing him on top of my head, he happily nuzzled into my hair and quickly fell asleep.

When John brought Shadow home, he was somewhat bemused to see a dove sound asleep on my head.

What next? he wondered.

Chapter 82
Hedgehogs

One summer evening, two large hedgehogs paid a visit, cuddling up together under the large patio bush. I filled a plate with meal-worms, which they happily devoured before wandering off to look for slugs. In the autumn, when the nights began to draw in, they settled down to hibernate below the decking, then reappeared in March.

After several years, our 'resident' hedgehog visitors disappeared. Perhaps they had found a new home or, sadly, died. The following year, spring floods completely filled our stream, overflowing into everyone's gardens. John heard that several young hedgehogs were seen wandering aimlessly around, in search of a home.

When John was out walking with Shadow, a friend stopped him and said she had found a baby hedgehog sprawled out on her lawn. She said he looked very weak and feeble and wondered if John could take it home. (She was aware I had once looked after new-born hedgehogs in France.)

By chance, we had recently purchased a hedgehog box. I quickly made a new home for the little one, filling the box with a selection of leaves, then scattering meal worms everywhere. First, I made sure the youngster had no injuries then gently put him inside the box.

I checked on him regularly, relieved he had quickly made himself at home and eaten most of the meal worms. Now, he was sound asleep. The next morning, John took the box down to the wild area, placing it below the decking. Lastly, he opened the little door so the hedgehog could come and go as he pleased.

Hopefully, when the little one woke up, he would soon meet up with his companions.

Would I ever see him again?

The following year, a hedgehog began wandering round the garden. Naturally, we offered him a plate of meal worms which he quickly gobbled up. Three months later, he was joined by a mate.

Once again, we now have a pair of hedgehogs arriving at dusk for their supper, occasionally bringing baby along too.

I named the adult hedgehogs Tammy and Toby, in memory of the tiny babies I nurtured in France.

Chapter 83
A New Family Member

In September 2020, I suggested to John that we look for a young budgerigar. (Seeing Jasper's empty cage in the garage always reduced me to tears.) After searching through various bird sites, we found a well-renowned pet shop. I made contact and was delighted to hear they had several birds for sale. The owner confirmed there were some budgerigars amongst the hatchlings. However, it would be another six weeks before these birds could be sold.

After the allotted time, we visited the shop. I asked the manager if there was a 'male' budgerigar amongst the fledglings. He said it was difficult to tell, as the colour of their ceres were not fully established. I asked if there was a blue bird amongst the brood. He nodded and went upstairs.

When the owner returned, he was carrying a small cage. Looking carefully at the bird, I noted its cere had the tiniest hint of mauve and, from previous experience, was convinced this hue would turn blue—indicating a male. I particularly wanted a boy as males are gentler and more inclined to speak than female birds.

I put my finger alongside the cage. This tiny bird immediately ran along his spar and began nibbling my pinkie.

I was totally smitten. Something in my heart whispered that he was going to be a beautiful and amazing bird.

After we had completed the sale and bought some food and numerous toys, the little one was put in an aerated box for the journey home. Sadly, the weather was horrendous—gales, wind and driving rain lashed us from all angles. It was a slow and arduous trip (very similar to the journey home in France, after buying Whisper/Shadow).

To keep the wee lad steady, I held him firmly on my knee, talking constantly to reassure him. John asked if I had come up with a name. I had been thinking about this while we were in the shop and suggested we call him 'Jamie'.

My late father was called Jimmy and my brother, who died at the age of ten from myeloid leukaemia—just six weeks after I was born—was called James. A fitting way of remembering Dad and my brother as they both adored birds.

Chapter 84
Jamie

Eventually, we arrived home, tired and exhausted by the journey. I brought Jamie into the kitchen where his cage was waiting. It had already been thoroughly cleaned and embellished with a mirror and a trio of bells. I quickly put Jamie into his cage.

The first thing we noticed was that Jasper's large cage would need some adaptation. Jamie was so tiny and, without more spars and extra ladders, he would be unable to access his food and water dishes.

While John was making the necessary adjustments, I held Jamie close to my chest, constantly repeating his name. He started making little chirping noises, then began nibbling my fingers.

After a few days, I brought Jamie out of his cage and encouraged him play with various toys I had arranged on the dining table. First, he was very nervous then very gradually began to nudge around his plastic ball. Later that week, Jamie was delighted when he managed to push all his toys onto the floor.

Teaching him to fly was a bit more difficult. His first attempts ended up with him tumbling to the floor. Gently picking him up and murmuring words of reassurance, I persuaded him to try again.

Perseverance on both sides won the day. Eventually, Jamie began flying with ease around the dining room. A few days later, we introduced him to the conservatory. (To stop him crashing into the windows, John had put more decal stickers on the glass.)

However, Jamie had a few accidents when he misjudged where he wanted to land. Picking him up, I always checked there were no injuries. Usually, a kiss and some reassuring words were all that was needed to soothe him.

In time, he started flying with ease from his cage through to the sitting room. He loved sitting on the back of the sofa, just as Jasper had done, watching cars and people passing by.

Chapter 85
Jamie Starts to Talk

Three months later, I was convinced Jamie was trying to speak. Previously, during playtime, his favourite perch was sitting on my finger, leaning against my cheek. He always pressed his beak against my lips when I began my chatter. What I failed to realise was that the vibration of my words against his beak was Jamie's way of absorbing his 'new' language. His first words were, 'Kiss, Kiss.'

From then on, he began mimicking everything he overheard. The following year, I thought Jamie was becoming bored with English and began teaching him French. He seemed to prefer the sound of French to English and soon began reeling off his new vocabulary. When guests visited, he would listen intently to their conversation and often repeated their chatter during his repertoire.

A few weeks before Christmas, I tried to teach him to say 'Bon Noel'. Strangely, he refused to comply. At playtime on Boxing Day, he flew onto my head and began his repertoire with, 'Merry Christmas, Birthday Boy!'

I wondered where he had picked this up. Later, I recalled that, before Christmas, one of our guests had greeted us with 'Merry Christmas'. Jamie had obviously been listening and preferred the sound of this phrase to 'Bon Noel'. (He also loved saying 'Birthday Boy', which was something I taught him prior to his first birthday.)

The following year, I introduced him to another romantic language—Italian. His first attempt was 'Ciao' (Hello or Goodbye). He then progressed to 'Mille Grazie' and 'Prego' (Many Thanks and You're Welcome).

When guests heard him chatting, they found it hard to believe that such a tiny bird had the ability to intertwine three languages—and do so with the right inflections!

Chapter 86
Jamie's Injuries

Sadly, Jamie had a few accidents during his first four years. First, he twisted his wing doing acrobatics on his swing. Later, he managed to damage his toe by tugging hard when one of his nails caught in a sofa cover. Happily, there was no lasting damage to the toe and, with the appropriate medication, he made a complete recovery. However, nothing can be done to fix his wing. Thankfully, Jamie adapted quickly to his flying limitations.

When he was two years old, we experienced a really frightening episode. Jamie began regurgitating all his seed. He was in a dreadful state. I was terrified he was going to die. The wee boy was in no state to be driven to the surgery. After a great deal of negotiation, we arranged for a home visit.

While we were waiting for a medic to arrive, Jamie sat on my finger, pressing his head against my cheek. Meanwhile, I was avidly watching the clock, counting the seconds till the vet was due.

As soon as he arrived, the vet took Jamie into his mobile van and gave him an injection, then orally administered antibiotics. We were told to put a few a few drops of this medication in his water dish every day for a week.

Thank heavens, the vet's diagnosis was spot-on. Jamie recovered well and within a few days, he began playing with his toys and chatting away in his various languages. (The trauma we experienced lasted many weeks!)

Jamie is a super wee chap—stubborn, determined and full of fun! He brightens our lives with his lively chatter and various antics. Every afternoon, I set out his playthings on the coffee table, before letting him out of his cage.

During playtime, his favourite game is to nudge the majority of his toys from the coffee table onto the floor, then begin tossing and chasing his plastic balls around the floor. (Just as Starsky did.)

Of course, we will never forget Jasper—or give up hope that he will be found. Every night I say a little prayer for his return, emphasising there is plenty of room in the conservatory for two cages.

Photo 13: Jamie at playtime

Chapter 87
Shadow Slows Down

Incredibly, Shadow could read my mind. I would only have to think of something—maybe I ought to brush her coat and clean her ears. I would ask Shadow to come into the kitchen and sit on her grooming towel. However, there was no need—when I turned around, Shadow was already sitting on her towel, waiting to be brushed. If I thought it necessary to hoover the sitting room (and she was lying in her bed in front of the fireplace), she would instinctively know what I wanted and move to her other bed in the conservatory.

She also recognised the engine noise our car made and never barked when we arrived home. However, if a neighbour or repairman arrived at our door, she would let the world know that someone was outside.

On the way home, after purchasing a new car, I mentioned to John that Shadow would probably react as if we were strangers. When we parked, there was no reaction from Shadow. How did she know it was us? With a new car, plus different engine sounds, I was convinced she would start barking.

Wrong again!

In her thirteenth year, Shadow became very arthritic. However, she still insisted on two daily walks and took every opportunity to enjoy a swim in Margam Lake.

During the summer, we arranged to see a (vet) physiotherapist. She taught Shadow how to do various exercises and gave us a detailed script of various manoeuvres she should practice at home. At first, Shadow was a bit reluctant to comply. In due course, she settled into a routine—exercises first, then a walk.

Sadly, by December, her appointments with the vet became more frequent and, on the run-up to Christmas, she appeared really sad and very downcast.

I took a few photos of Shadow sitting beside our Xmas tree in the conservatory. Shadow is gazing up at me—looking a little more content than previously. In my heart, I sensed my poor darling was not going to last long. Tears trickled down my cheeks. What would 2022 bring? I wiped my eyes, refusing to think too far ahead.

We tried to cheer up Shadow by taking her on short walks—her favourite spot was to amble along the promenade by the beach. When neighbours visited to share our festive fare, Shadow perked up considerably. Shadow loved having visitors, totally aware she would be indulged with various treats.

Chapter 88
Shadow and Sandy

Two months before Christmas, we were inveigled into buying a puppy. He is a lovely golden colour and befits his name—Sandy. Although adorable, he is a mischievous wee lad and up to all sorts of tricks.

It was really important to stop Sandy interacting too closely with Shadow. The arthritis in Shadow's front leg prevented her putting a paw on the puppy's neck when he jumped at her face. (A younger Shadow would have been agile enough to put a stop to such bad behaviour.)

Shadow made up her own mind on how to befriend the puppy. She would lean into his playpen so they could rub noses. Sandy loved this and would leap up and down, begging for more 'kisses'.

In February, we began taking Sandy for training lessons, hoping to exercise his mind and teach him good behaviour. He appeared to enjoy this new adventure. The trainer advised us to feed Sandy by hand instead of putting his food in a dish.

He loved this and our bonding strengthened.

Then a big problem reared its head. When we began reintroducing his meals in a bowl, he refused to eat anything. Then hand-feeding was also rejected. I tried tempting him with chicken and meat—nothing worked. John bought every dog-food available in the shops and occasionally some of the tinned food would be eaten, then later disdained.

We were frantic he would starve to death.

Shadow was very frail at this point and needed lots of attention too. One of my main worries was if/when we lost Shadow then Sandy would go into total meltdown.

In mid-March, after Shadow had been for her morning walk, John returned to the village to collect his newspaper. I asked Shadow to come inside. It was essential to let the puppy into the garden for his morning pee.

When Shadow refused to budge, I started to worry. This was out of character—she rarely refused any request. Shadow curled up on an old blanket by the garden gate and dropped off to sleep.

When John returned, Shadow followed him into the house. Now that Shadow was safely indoors, I let Sandy have a run in the garden. When he was exhausted, I put him back in his playpen, once more trying to entice him to eat something. Eventually, he swallowed two tiny morsels of meat.

Aware that Shadow's appetite had further diminished, I put together a small breakfast—cubes of steak, garnished with a piece of sausage. Shadow turned her head away and refused to eat anything. She sipped a little water, then curled up in her bed.

Now, I was frantic with worry. John telephoned the vet and requested an urgent appointment.

Chapter 89
Pain and Grief

John took Shadow to the surgery—I stayed at home, trying to console the puppy. Sandy was looking sad and forlorn, perhaps aware that something was amiss. Thirty minutes later, John telephoned. I could tell from his voice that the news was bad.

The vet's examination revealed that Shadow's tummy was very swollen and there was a strong possibility she had cancer. He was told to take Shadow to their main surgery, as she needed an urgent scan.

Later that morning, I had a call from John. The scan showed Shadow had two cancerous tumours in her stomach and another on her liver. The vet said an operation would not be tenable and pain-medication would provide only temporary relief. Sadly, the preferred recommendation was euthanasia.

As Shadow was in considerable pain, the vet said it would be a kindness to put her to sleep today. If she was allowed to come home, albeit for a short while, the slightest bump would cause her to bleed to death. This would be horribly painful for Shadow and tragic for us to witness.

Shadow had now been given strong painkillers to alleviate some of her torment.

Choking back tears, I turned my attention to Sandy. I encouraged him to eat a few morsels of food, then let him have a run in the garden, before settling him into his playpen. I also hid some treats under his bed, knowing he would soon sniff them out. Sandy quickly dropped off to sleep, cuddled up to his beloved teddy.

Now, I could prepare myself for the ordeal ahead. Lots of memories flooded my mind and tears were already trickling down my cheeks. A few minutes later, I heard John's car arriving and rushed outside. On the way to the vet, I tentatively asked John about the best way to cope with the ordeal which lay ahead.

Nothing sprang to mind.

After more thought, we concluded the only solution was to keep calm and comfort our beloved dog during her final moments.

Chapter 90
Adieu, Ma Petite

When we arrived at the practice, we were shown into a little room. There was a small blanket folded up on the counter, which I spread on the floor. We waited impatiently for Shadow.

Every second we were apart seemed like a century.

Through the partially-opened door, I caught a glimpse of Shadow, dragging the vet towards the exit—she presumed she was going home! The painkillers had obviously helped. Shadow's instincts knew we were nearby. Seeing me standing by the door, she tugged her lead from the vet's hand and bounded straight towards us. Unprompted, Shadow lay down on the blanket, her beautiful brown eyes staring bemusedly at our tear-stained cheeks.

We gently caressed her, constantly telling her how much she was loved. Shadow was somewhat confused—I was always hugging her but John usually shied away from giving cuddles.

Ten minutes later, the vet arrived. She told us Shadow had recently been given a tranquiliser.

I cradled Shadow's head, kissing her softly, while John gently stroked her back. We quietly murmured our fond farewells. At one point, Shadow raised her head, licked the tears from my eyes, then gave me a gentle kiss on the lips.

This was so special as Shadow normally shied away from giving kisses.

A few minutes later, the vet administered the euthanasia. More tears dropped on Shadow's head as the light faded from her eyes. I held her close to my chest and prayed so hard for her passing to be gentle. A few moments later, the vet whispered, 'Shadow has gone.'

Chapter 91
Coping with Grief

It was a quiet and tearful journey home. The pain of losing Shadow left us reeling. How would we cope with the coming weeks? Deep in our hearts, we knew we had to be strong—the puppy would quickly tune into our anxiety if we looked anxious and stressed.

Unable to explain to Sandy that Shadow would not be coming home, we tried to stick to his normal routine. However, he knew something was wrong and was very unsettled. Putting on a brave face and stirring my inner strength, I began preparing dinner. I suggested to John that he should take Sandy for a little walk to calm him down.

Later, we played a game of Scrabble, trying hard not to focus on Shadow's demise. Sandy was now curled up in bed, fast asleep. Fortunately, his walk, some tiny morsels of food, plus a few games had totally exhausted him. Hopefully, tomorrow he would be more settled.

The following morning, we showed Sandy Shadow's empty bed in the conservatory. We let him sniff the scent which still lingered there and have a little mooch around. Suddenly, he leapt towards the sill and snatched a miniature black labrador from the surround. Running back to his playpen, he hid this 'prize' under his bed. A strange reaction from a little puppy.

It was a particularly sad day when it was time to collect Shadow's ashes. Holding that little wooden box, knowing this was all that remained of our fantastic friend and loyal companion, reduced both of us to tears.

After some debate, we decided to buy two wall-mounted pots and put Shadow's ashes in one and those from Tinkerbelle and Blondi in the other. (As the latter were inseparable, I am sure they would have been happy with this.) I planted some lovely dianthus, called pink kisses, in both pots and the beautiful scent wafts over us when we are sitting on the patio.

Photo 14: Lizzie staring at Shadow's wall planter

Chapter 92
Poem of Remembrance

The lady who ran the grooming parlour had been very enamoured of Shadow. She frequently told us Shadow was a model 'patient'. Apparently, she used to outshine all the other dogs on how to behave when being groomed and having her nails clipped.

When Sandy was first booked in for a bath, we wondered what his response would be. His initial reaction was to stand stock-still and resist being taken into the parlour. Then he began whining. Fortunately, this fear quickly evaporated when he realised the staff would indulge him with lots of treats. On subsequent occasions, he bounded into the parlour and began plying the staff with oodles of 'kisses'.

The following month, when John brought Sandy back from the groomers, he gave me several 'dog poems' Jan had received from various friends. Most were tales concerning the loss of a dog.

Reading through them, a particular poem struck a chord. I truly believe these words (with a little annotation) crystallise the essence of Shadow's spirit.

If It Should Be

If one day I seem in pain,
And at night I cannot sleep,
Then you must do what must be done.
This last battle cannot be won.

You will be sad, I feel your grief.
Do not let your tears sway my needs.
For on this day, more than all the rest
Your love for me must stand the test.

We've had so many happy years
That what's to come can hold no fears.
I am in pain and suffering so.
It's now the time to let me go.

Take me where my pain will melt,
Yet please stay with me till the end.
Hold me close and speak to me
Until my eyes no longer see.

Such love as ours will never die.
So say farewell, and not goodbye.
Remember we will meet again.

Adieu Maman, Adieu Papa

Adieu Petite

Chapter 93
A Twist in the Tale

Before I finish this story, there is a little twist to the tale. I decided to purchase a chain, intending to attach this to Shadow's 'nametag'. This way, Shadow would always stay close to my heart.

After searching through several jewellers, we eventually found the perfect chain. During our shopping expedition, I kept thinking about all the photos we had of Shadow, particularly those taken in France and Lampeter. (These photos were apparently on an old disc and John promised he would try to input them onto our new computer.)

I recalled a particular snap where Shadow was sitting proudly beside the 'real' football we bought for her third birthday. This ball brought Shadow so much joy. Even when it became moth-eaten and rather tatty, it was her one and only 'toy'.

When we returned from our shopping expedition, John spent several hours on the computer as he was anxious to find details he needed for a work project.

After downloading these papers, John was amazed to see some old photos of Shadow had mysteriously materialised.

Amongst these snapshots, I was overjoyed to see the particular photos of Shadow I was keen to attach to my story.

However, it was a little mystifying as to why these snaps suddenly appeared. I wondered if Shadow had waved her magic wand—just like the true artiste she had always been!

I always wear Shadow's nametag and, because it glistens, it has become a source of attraction for Jamie. When he is out for playtime, he frequently flies onto my head and scrambles down towards the tag. Clinging on tightly, he begins his chatter. For some reason, his first word is 'Papa'. Later, he flies onto my head and reels off his favourite phrases, always bringing tears to my eyes when he says, 'Where's Shadow?'

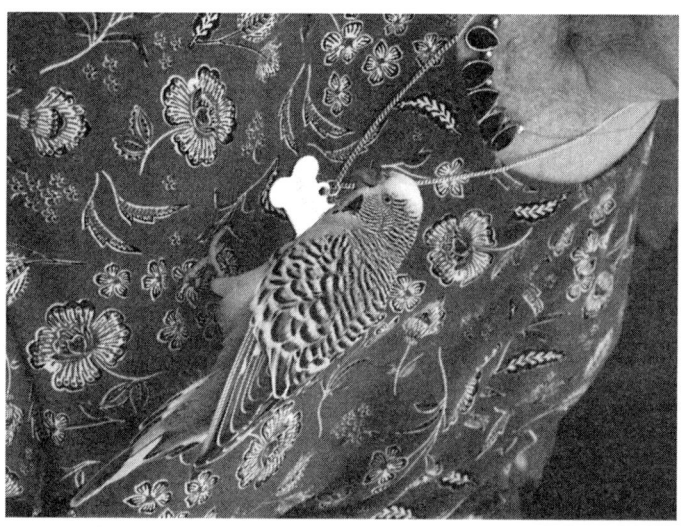

Photo 15: Jamie talking to Shadow's nametag

Chapter 94
Sandy and Food

In September, we rented a holiday cottage in Scotland, hoping the extra walks and excitement of going on holiday would stimulate the puppy's appetite. For two weeks, apart from nibbling at a piece of haddock, Sandy ate nothing.

The night we arrived home, Sandy collapsed on the floor. We tried giving him puppy food and dog biscuits. Reluctantly, he ate a few mouthfuls of food but rejected the biscuits. The next day we took him to the vet. Checking his weight, she said Sandy had lost two kilos. However, she could find nothing seriously amiss and her only advice was to keep trying different brands of dog-food and biscuits. If he appeared to show interest in anything we cooked, we should try giving him a piece to taste.

Later that week, I cooked a whole chicken. When I took it from the oven to cool, Sandy began to whine. I tried giving him a piece of white meat, which he rejected. John then gave him a bit of brown meat from the leg, which he pounced on and gobbled the lot. That night, he ate a whole leg of chicken.

At last, we had turned a corner. However, he also needed to eat nutritious dog biscuits. So far, he had rejected every single packet we had bought—there was already a bin, full of biscuits, in the garage which we planned to donate to a dog rescue centre.

John searched the internet and eventually discovered a new biscuit on the market 'guaranteed to be loved by any dog'.

Would Sandy be the exception? I wondered.

Amazingly, these biscuits got top marks from our little terror.

Today, Sandy's breakfast is half a chicken leg, embellished with a small piece of liver and carrot. In the evening, he is satisfied with his new biscuits, garnished with small pieces of meat, followed by a few treats.

It took ten worrying months to solve the puzzle of a dog who refused to eat.

Chapter 95
Living with Sandy

Sandy now plays a big part in our life. He adores going for his daily walks, especially when we take a picnic to Margam Park. First, he has to visit the donkeys and is mesmerised when we feed them handfuls of chopped carrots. A recent addition to the park are alpacas which have become a great attraction for visitors. One day, a young alpaca leant over his fence and licked Sandy's head. At first our puppy was totally mesmerised, then delighted, by this strange encounter.

One day John took Sandy for an extra-long walk, taking him to a good vantage spot where he could view his surroundings. Sandy sat stock-still looking at everything—the nearby hills and all the sheep. He also had a distant view of the Bristol Channel. Sandy stared at 'his world' for a long time, slowly rotating his head from side to side.

When they arrived home, John explained what had happened. He said Sandy appeared to be absorbing and memorising everything, almost as if he had a small camera in his head.

During the spring, Sandy spotted some new-born lambs when they were crossing a field. John kept him on a tight leash, worried the puppy might scare the wee ones. He was also acutely aware of the mothers, keeping a watchful eye on their offspring. Bizarrely, Sandy sat and watched the lambs, showing no inclination to chase them. Sandy can also be a little terror and, in spite of all our efforts, many faults still need correction. He tends to bark hysterically when the postman puts a letter through our front door. Fortunately, we heard about anti-bark collars and Sandy wears one every morning. This does him no harm and only sprays a little citrus juice in the air, which stops his morning tantrum.

He also adores 'stealing'. If a paper napkin or pen is left too near the edge of the kitchen table, it quickly disappears and anything, accidentally dropped, is promptly snatched away. On dry days, Sandy buries his 'trophy'—often John's slipper—in the garden. If it is raining, his prize gets hidden somewhere in the house, usually under his bed. Hopefully, one day, he will grow out of this behaviour as our reprimands have no effect. Now, a different trainer has taken on the task of teaching Sandy obedience. We wish him luck!

Sandy also has many good points. He is loving and gentle, does not bite or bear grudges, and adores giving 'kisses'. After dinner, we cuddle up together on the sofa. This is our favourite time of day. I give him some treats then we snuggle up together, watching television.

Peace at last!

Photo 16: Sandy

Although Shadow and Sandy only had a short time together, I strongly believe Shadow imbued her love of all animals into Sandy.

I also think she is keeping a watchful eye on the puppy and trying to steer him in the direction of becoming yet another 'superstar'!

The End

Summary
For the Love of Animals

This story concerns the great joy (and sadness) brought into our lives by the many pets John and I have looked after throughout the years. Shadow—originally called Whisper—is the main character. It took several years for Shadow to overcome the terrors of her dreadful start in life. To our great joy, she evolved into a faithful, wise and obedient dog. Her main aim in life was to love and be loved by everyone.

Sandy is the latest addition to the family and there are some similarities to Shadow—he is friendly towards people and all animals. More importantly, he adores being loved.

Like all puppies, he can be disobedient. However, Sandy is always forgiven and reciprocates with lots of gentle kisses!